I'm Not Just Gifted

I'm Not Just Gifted

SOCIAL-EMOTIONAL CURRICULUM FOR GUIDING GIFTED CHILDREN

CHRISTINE FONSECA

PRUFROCK PRESS INC.

WACO, TEXAS

DEDICATION

Dedicated to the teachers, counselors, and support staff who strive to help gifted children reach their potential through their social and emotional development.

Library of Congress Cataloging-in-Publication Data

Fonseca, Christine, 1966-
 I'm not just gifted : social-emotional curriculum for guiding gifted children / by Christine Fonseca.
    pages cm
 Includes bibliographical references.
 ISBN 978-1-61821-425-6 (pbk.)
 1. Gifted children--Education. 2. Gifted children--Education--Curricula. 3. Social skills in children--Study and teaching. 4. Emotions in children--Study and teaching. I. Title.
 LC3993.F67 2015
 371.95--dc23
                          2015006442

At the time of this book's publication, all facts and figures cited are the most current available. All telephone numbers, addresses, and website URLs are accurate and active. All publications, organizations, websites, and other resources exist as described in the book, and all have been verified. The author and Prufrock Press Inc. make no warranty or guarantee concerning the information and materials given out by organizations or content found at websites, and we are not responsible for any changes that occur after this book's publication. If you find an error, please contact Prufrock Press Inc.

Prufrock Press Inc.
P.O. Box 8813
Waco, TX 76714-8813
Phone: (800) 998-2208
Fax: (800) 240-0333
http://www.prufrock.com

Table of Contents

ACKNOWLEDGEMENTS

It was more than a privilege to bring this book to you, and it would not have been possible without the help of the people on this list.

To Lacy Compton and the team at Prufrock Press—This was your brain child. Thank you for trusting me to bring it to life.

To my writing partner, Michelle McLean—I really have no words. You always manage to find time to read and give your two cents. I wouldn't be the author I am today without you!

To my RL BFFs and cheer squad: Jodi, Kelley, Nancy, Jill, Corrine, Joe, and Andrea—I know none of you realize how much our regular convos help me with this vocation of mine!

To my GT support online, Deborah, Jen, and Lisa—Your shared insights into the world of gifted children have sparked much of who I am and what I do. Thank you for what you give back every day.

To the gifted children who have blessed my life throughout the years—This book really is for you. Your daily words and struggles, your insight and wisdom—these are the things that have shaped the lessons in this book. It is with your unique perspective and vision that I've created every page. THANK YOU for the inspiration you so freely share with the world.

Finally, my acknowledgements are never complete without a personal thank you to my family, both immediate and extended:

To Dirck, Fabiana, and Erika—I never grow tired of telling you all how much you mean to me. My vocation occurs because of your unyielding support and willingness to share me with my words.

To my extended family—Thanks for the daily reminders to stay balanced. I'm certain I'd be so much less without you in my life.

—Christine Fonseca

INTRODUCTION

As a practicing school psychologist and life coach who specializes in understanding the often hidden social and emotional lives of gifted children, I see the direct impact affective curriculum has on the emotional development of children. It is from this place that I bring to you this book. Gifted children need caring individuals who can help them with self-awareness, emotional intelligence, resiliency, and talent development. Without coaching in these areas, many of our gifted youth grow up believing they are destined to be misfits and outcasts. This is untrue. Gifted individuals can find their place within the world, without sacrificing their cognitive prowess. They can develop strong friendships, reduce the impact of their asynchronous development, and appreciate the more unique aspects of their personality.

This book was designed to develop the social and emotional lives of gifted youth. Written as 30-minute lessons that can be done in small- or whole-group instruction, *I'm Not Just Gifted* joins current research regarding the social and emotional development of gifted children with evidence-based counseling and coaching practices and educational standards from the National Association of Gifted Children (NAGC), State Learning Standards to Advance Social and Emotional Learning (SEL), and Common Core State Standards (CCSS) practices. It is my hope that teachers and counselors alike will find ways to incorporate this affective curriculum into the normal educational experience and enhance the social and emotional lives of our gifted youth.

Section I
Overview and Essential Understanding

CHAPTER 1

Understanding the Social and Emotional Lives of Gifted Children

A Primer

Giftedness is more than high performance on a standardized intelligence test (Renzulli, 1978). It is a collection of talents and traits affecting all aspects of a person—from cognition to personality to social-emotional development (Webb, Gore, Amend, & DeVries, 2007). With recent advances in neuroscience, researchers in the field of giftedness have replaced old beliefs about cognition and emotional development as somewhat fixed and static to theories that incorporate a strong developmental aspect to giftedness, influenced by the environment and the development of identity (Renzulli, 2005; Gagné, 2005; Moon, 2009). It is from this perspective that this book was created.

Gifted children have unique social and emotional traits that influence their life experiences. These characteristics can be shaped and influenced by the support we offer (Moon, 2009). And what better place than within the classroom setting?

But more on that in a minute. First, I want to review the most recent research regarding the common social-emotional characteristics of gifted children and how these impact their overall functioning.

Hébert (2011), drawing on the work of researchers over the past two decades, highlights several specific social-emotional traits that most influence a gifted child's life. Development of appropriate supports for their social and emotional lives can not be considered without first having an understanding of these traits.

HIGH PERFORMANCE STANDARDS

Gifted children often hold themselves and others to impossibly high standards. Although having high performance standards is not a bad quality, it can become a problem for gifted children when the need to perform at a high level morphs into an unhealthy perfectionism, resulting in everything from severe procrastination, to extreme mood swings dependent on the gifted child's perception of meeting his or her personal expectations. Teachers can help gifted children learn to embrace their high standards and learn to not hold others to the same, often unrealistic, expectations (Silverman, 2007).

INTERNAL MOTIVATION

Hébert (2011) cited internal motivation as being one of the constants in gifted education literature. Internal motivation is the ability of an individual to overcome personal adversity and stay focused on his or her goals. Strengthening this trait can protect against the negative impact of anxiety and bolster overall resiliency.

EMOTIONAL INTENSITY

I've written much on the topic of emotional intensity. In my view, as well as that of much of the research in this area, emotional intensity and sensitivity is a cornerstone aspect of giftedness. Emotional intensity involves students' deep, sometimes overwhelming emotional sensitivity to themselves and the world around them (Fonseca, 2011b). Characterized by intense highs and lows, gifted children who experience this level of sensitivity can be easily hurt emotionally. Likewise, they will often be overly self-critical if they hurt another person emotionally (Hébert, 2011). Teaching gifted children about the positive aspects of intensity can help prevent the more negative impact of this level of sensitivity.

EMPATHY

In addition to emotional intensity, gifted children often experience high levels of empathy. Current research in the field of gifted education suggests that these levels of empathy are leading to stronger levels of social concern (Reis & Renzulli, 2004). This matches my experience with gifted children, many of whom express concerns with major world issues including war, the global economy, and conservation, to name a few. Researchers including Renzulli (2009) and others are calling on educators to look for more ways to encourage the social awareness present in our gifted youth.

MORAL MATURITY

Researchers have long identified advanced moral maturity with giftedness in children (Hébert, 2011). Gifted people demonstrate the ability to use advanced moral judgment even when faced with peer pressure to engage in acts that compromise their values. This internalization of morals enables gifted youths to conform to their internal code even in difficult situations. Support for the acquisition and strengthening of this moral maturity will only enhance this skill, especially within the school setting.

SELF-ACTUALIZATION

Although the research in this area is somewhat sparse, there appears to be evidence that gifted youth have a strong desire or need for self-actualization (Hébert, 2011). Certainly my own anecdotal information from working with gifted children over the past two decades confirms this perspective. Gifted children are driven toward self-actualization at a young age and when this need is not met, existential depression can result (Webb et al., 2007).

RESILIENCE

Similar to internal motivation, resilience is a highly researched construct that has been linked to giftedness (Reis & Renzulli, 2004). Often defined as the ability to bounce back after a setback, resilient children often demonstrate similar skills to gifted children, including intellectual curiosity, internal motivation, and strong problem-solving skills (Hébert, 2011). Nurturing and developing resiliency in gifted children can serve as a significant protection factor against not only environmental barriers, but also the negative impact of anxiety and emotional distress.

The traits outlined above represent the most significant and consistent social-emotional characteristics in the literature. Understanding these particular traits opens the door to the development of an affective curriculum that can enhance the lives of gifted children. Moreover, analysis of these traits and more importantly, how to support them, can guide the process of developing appropriate social-emotional curriculum for gifted children.

CHAPTER 2

The Case for Affective Curriculum

One of the most exciting recent fields of research in psychology is the positive psychology movement. This field of study takes the link between emotions and their influence on thinking and behavior and combines it with the concept of nurturing positivity instead of focusing on maladaptive behaviors. It is the study of optimism and mental "wellness" (Olenchak, 2009).

The tenants of positive psychology have interesting implications for gifted students and the state of gifted education. Founded in the ideas of optimism, hope, and "flow," positive psychology purports that when a person is taught how to be happy and hopeful, and is provided with opportunities to be fully immersed and energized by what he or she is doing, the person will develop personal excellence and experience fulfillment in his or her life. When applied to gifted children, this means that in order for gifted children to truly benefit from their education and develop personal excellence, they must be given access to enriching curriculum, both for academics and affective skill development (Olenchak, 2009), something that happens inconsistently at best. Creating stimulating affective curriculum that encompasses the development of emotional intelligence and talent development can help to bridge this need (Jung, 2012).

Research examining the link between affective skill development and academic achievement for all students confirms something most educators have felt—emotional intelligence, even more than cognitive ability, influences academic performance (Durlak, Weissberg, Dymnicki, Taylor, & Schellinger, 2010). However, research related to gifted education highlights an even more significant need for gifted individuals to receive support for their social and emotional development (Neihart, Reis,

Robinson, & Moon, 2002). Through the development and delivery of appropriate affective curriculum, gifted children can harness their numerous gifts and potential.

For affective curriclulum to be most effective, it cannot be a reactive model of correcting or "fixing" perceived problems experienced by gifted individuals. It should be carefully designed and embedded into the very fabric of education. Not only should gifted children be given opportunities to deepen their study of various academic topics, but they should be allowed and encouraged to think about their feelings related to that content, link the information to their interests, and develop actionable responses. In doing this, their social-emotional traits are not only supported, but developed and embraced. This, in turn, leads to optimum maturation and the ability to harness their potential.

As someone who works closely with teachers on a daily basis, I know fully embedding affective curriculum is not often possible within the framework of traditional education. The mini-lessons in this book were developed as a starting point for classroom teachers, counselors, and psychologists to use as schools move in the direction of understanding, valuing, and embracing affective education for our gifted youth.

CHAPTER 3

Embedding Affective Curriculum Into the Classroom

Now that the reason for using affective curriculum in the school setting is clear, it is important to discuss how to embed the curriculum into the classroom. Affective curriculum is usually introduced in one of three ways: proactive, reactive, and integrative. Proactive approaches focus on developing the skills necessary to facilitate personal growth and development. Reactive strategies happen in response to problems that interfere with learning. Integrative practices focus on attending to affective components of instruction and activities (Peterson, 2009). As I mentioned previously, reactive responses are not optimal, although they can have some limited benefit. In my experience, a combination of proactive and integrative approaches minimizes the future need to develop reactive strategies.

Regardless of which approach is taken, it is important to focus on where the student is currently, not where we assume the student *should* be (Peterson, 2009). Maintaining focus on the present enables educators to create safe, nonjudgmental environments. These types of environments are necessary for any type of affective curriculum delivery. Furthermore, accepting students at their current functional levels enables educators to focus on strengths and build autonomy.

COMPONENTS

Current research has indicated several components of an effective social-emotional curriculum program. These components include self-assessment, defining "meaning," talent development, emotional intelligence development, and the use of bibliotherapy. This type of programming also points to the need for proactive, deliberate planning with consideration of both cognitive and emotional development (VanTassel-Baska, 2009). Let's examine each of these components more closely.

Self-assessment refers to the understanding of aptitude, interest, and general personality traits. Use of standardized measures, as well as strategies to explore self-evaluation, should be incorporated into any affective curriculum program. Creating "meaning" in one's life is a natural outflow of self-assessment. Creating purpose and linking that to current experiences comes after an understanding of interests and aptitude. A strong social-emotional curriculum program will involve both self-assessment and talent development. Lessons that link interests and talent development to this greater concept of "meaning" should begin at a young age in order to have the greatest impact.

Typically defined as the ability to perceive emotions, understand emotions, and regulate emotions, emphasizing emotional intelligence enables gifted students to develop strength in the core social-emotional competencies (VanTassel-Baska, 2009). Lessons in this domain can include developing an understanding of emotions and personal emotional reactions, as well as applying emotional understanding to cognitive reasoning. Embedding emotional content into typical classroom settings could be as easy as using stories to interpret emotional reactions from characters as well as motivation. Bibliotherapy, in particular, can be effectively used to build emotional intelligence skills. More about this technique can be found later in this chapter.

The lessons presented in this book provide specific ways to address the components listed here. Self-assessment, talent development, personal guidance, and emotional intelligence are all addressed through the lessons. Using evidence-based strategies that include journaling, visual/performing arts activities, and writing or oral communication, these lessons highlight a variety of ways to address the social-emotional needs of gifted students (Olszewski-Kubilius & Thomson, 2015; Peterson & Lorimer, 2011; VanTassel-Baska, Buckingham, & Baska, 2009). Additional ideas for embedding these components within the curriculum can be found in the section below. These examples go beyond the 30-minute lessons, allowing for educators to create broader levels of depth and student involvement.

SPECIFIC STRATEGIES

The following evidence-based strategies are effective ways to enhance the social-emotional development of gifted children while providing academic content. They capitalize on an integrative model and focus on the affective content within curriculum and activities. What I particularly like about these strategies is the ability for an educator (teacher, counselor, psychologist) to be able to develop emotional intelligence and other important socioemotional skills while continuing to meet grade-level standards. I also like how adaptable these activities are, enabling educators to meet the developmental needs of children.

BIBLIOTHERAPY

Referring to the use of stories to teach emotional skills, bibliotherapy is something used in mental health arenas and school settings. Using books to teach and explore everything from social problems to emotional intelligence, bibliotherapy is a highly effective tool for an affective curriculum program (Halsted, 2009). Teachers can use stories in a structured way, incorporating emotionally based questions into the analysis of the text. Unstructured use of bibliotherapy involves the availability of appropriate stories in school and classroom libraries for student use. Journal assignments related to free reading choices can bring out the affective content of the book through self-reflection questions.

BIOGRAPHY

Similar to bibliotherapy, biography refers to the use of biographical stories to help students develop affective skills and solve personal problems (Hébert, 2009). In this strategy, the bibliotherapy is focused on stories of other gifted individuals with similar cultural backgrounds and interests as the students. The platform provides insight as students begin to self-assess. Using discussion-style groups can draw out strong emotional connections between the reader and personal experiences.

VIDEOTHERAPY

Another strategy similar to bibliotherapy is videotherapy. In this technique, books are replaced by film media. The goal is self-discovery as students view films based on particular affective goals. Discussion group techniques coupled with the viewing can make this a particularly powerful strategy for encouraging self-assessment (VanTassel-Baska et al., 2009). Hébert (2011) offered an extensive list of biographies helpful with both bibliotherapy and videotherapy.

VISUAL/PERFORMING ARTS INSTRUCTION

The use of visual and performing arts is nothing new in the therapeutic process. Here, the use of art instruction within the school setting is purposefully built to incorporate many aspects of affective curriculum into everyday programming. Many gifted children use art, both visual and performing, as a way to express themselves at an early age. Formal instruction in the arts provides a platform to teach everything from understanding the connection between emotion and artistic expression, the connection between culture and emotional expressions, and self-assessment from an artistic point of view.

I've provided many examples of how affective curriculum can be embedded into the academic environment, both as short-term mini lessons and full, enriching experiences. As you work through the lessons in this book, you'll be able to see how to incorporate many of the extension and enrichment strategies. I've even provided a few specific examples of how to expand on the topics and lessons provided. Regardless of which strategies you use, I hope that you will begin to integrate affective skill development into your daily practice.

CHAPTER 4

Evidence-Based Design and Lesson Overview

This book was designed to be used with small groups of gifted students set up like discussion groups. This methodology was selected in order to place equal focus on both process and output. Furthermore, discussion groups will provide the gifted students opportunities to connect with like-minded peers and learn the various social-emotional concepts within a safe setting (Peterson, Betts, & Bradley, 2009).

Lessons are structured to incorporate activites and discussion periods, drawing on the best practices outlined by both Peterson's structured model of discussion and Bradley's more creative approach. Activities presented with the lessons are relatively short, but easily adaptable to longer extension activities if desired. Each lesson ties into a variety of national standards, including the National Association for Gifted Children (NAGC, 2010) standards, the Collaborative for Academic, Social, and Emotional Learning (CASEL, n.d.) social-emotional learning core competencies, and the Common Core State Standards for English Language Arts (National Governors Association Center for Best Practices & Council of Chief State School Officers, 2010). Table 1 (see p. 15) specifies the specific standards utilized in the development of these lessons. It is my hope that by linking the lessons to these standards, teachers will be afforded opportunities to weave affective curriculum into their weekly practices more effectively and consistently.

HOW TO USE THIS BOOK

As already mentioned, the lessons in this book are based on a discussion group format. It seems appropriate, then, to discuss how to group students in order to achieve the goals of these lessons. To begin with, gifted students should be grouped homogeneously based on age as much as possible. This is due to the unique social and emotional development of students at various ages. Combining several age or grade groups into a single discussion group can be difficult and could negatively impact the group as a whole (Peterson et al., 2009). In my own practice, I have grouped fourth- and fifth-grade students together using an additional adult to facilitate a group within a group. Another important consideration when forming groups is the length of time for the groups. The lessons in this book were designed to be completed in 30-minute increments on average. Setting a specific number of lessons for each discussion group to accomplish could enable the facilitator to maintain a closed membership once the groups begin. Additional interested members could join the next session of groups when they begin.

In addition to the specific considerations for the set up of discussion groups, it is important for educators to set norms regarding confidentiality and expected behavior at the start of the group. This can help establish a safe environment in which the lessons can be conducted.

LESSON OVERVIEW

The lessons in this book are set up in units, each focusing on a specific aspect of social and emotional development. Each unit begins with a brief overview followed by lessons and supplemental materials. Unit I focuses on the definition of giftedness and inherent expectations related to the "gifted" label. Lessons are designed to help facilitate an understanding of the specific traits of giftedness and foster self-awareness. Unit II centers around emotional intelligence, focusing on self-awareness, managing emotions, and conflict resolution. These skills form the foundation of emotional intelligence and set the stage for future skill development. Unit III is about creating a strong foundation for the development of social and emotional skills. Optimism, positive self-talk, motivation, responsibility, and appropriate decision-making skills are addressed. Unit IV covers resiliency, including adaptive, relationship, communication, and leadership skills. The book concludes with Unit V, focusing on talent development. The constructs of goal-setting and career guidance are explored in this unit.

In addition to the brief overview at the start of each unit, suggestions are provided for extension and enrichment opportunities based on the types of learning opportunities discussed in Chapter 3. This provides educators with an opportunity to dive deeper into topics of interest. Table 1 presents each lesson and the appropriate standards linked to the lesson. Educators are encouraged to choose the lessons appropriate for the goals and objectives of each group.

Table 1. Index of Lessons

LESSON	SEL COMPETENCY	NAGC STANDARDS	CCSS STANDARDS
Unit 1			
Lesson 1: The Meaning of Giftedness (p. 23)	Self-awareness	1.1 Self-Understanding 1.2 Self-Understanding	W.4 SL.6
Lesson 2: Not Just Gifted (p. 27)	Self-awareness Social-awareness Relationship skills	1.1 Self-Understanding 1.2 Self-Understanding 1.3 Self-Understanding	SL.5 SL.6
Lesson 3: Great Expectations (p. 30)	Self-awareness Relationship skills	1.1 Self-Understanding 1.2 Self-Understanding 1.7 Cognitive and Affective Growth 3.2 Talent Development	W.3 W.4 W.6 L.1
Lesson 4: The Story of My Life (p. 33)	Self-awareness Self-management	1.7 Cognitive and Affective Growth 1.8 Cognitive and Affective Growth 4.1 Personal Competence	W.4 W.6
Unit II			
Lesson 5: Soaring With Strengths (p. 37)	Self-awareness	1.2 Self-Understanding 4.1 Personal Competence 4.5 Communication Competence	SL.3 SL.4 SL.6
Lesson 6: Am I Afraid? (p. 41)	Self-awareness Self-management	1.1 Self-Understanding 4.1 Personal Competence	W.4 SL.1 SL.6
Lesson 7: Being Mindful (p. 44)	Self-management	4.1 Personal Competence 4.3 Leadership	SL.6
Lesson 8: Understanding Emotions (p. 47)	Self-management	1.1 Self-Understanding 4.1 Personal Competence 4.2 Social Competence	W.4 SL.6
Lesson 9: My Emotional Vocabulary (p. 51)	Self-awareness Self-management	1.1 Self-Understanding 4.1 Personal Competence	W.4 L.1 L.6
Lesson 10: My Hula Hoop (p. 54)	Self-awareness Self-management Social-awareness	1.3 Self-Understanding 4.1 Personal Competence 4.2 Social Competence	SL.6
Lesson 11: Understanding Triggers (p. 57)	Self-awareness Self-management Relationship skills	4.1 Personal Competence 4.2 Social Competence	W.4 SL.1 SL.5
Lesson 12: How Mad Am I? (p. 60)	Self-awareness Self-management Relationship skills	4.1 Personal Competence 4.2 Social Competence 4.5 Communication Competence	W.4 SL.6
Lesson 13: Being a Creative Problem Solver (p. 63)	Relationship skills Responsible decision-making	3.4 Instructional Strategies 4.1 Personal Competence 4.2 Social Competence	W.4 SL.6
Unit III			
Lesson 14: The Person in the Mirror (p. 69)	Self-awareness Self-management	1.1 Self-Understanding 1.2 Self-Understanding 4.1 Personal Competence	W.3 W.4 L.1 L.6

Table 1. Continued

LESSON	SEL COMPETENCY	NAGC STANDARDS	CCSS STANDARDS
Lesson 15: I Think I Can (p. 73)	Self-awareness Self-management	1.2 Self-Understanding 4.1 Personal Competence	W.2 W.4 W.6
Lesson 16: I'm Proud of . . . (p. 77)	Self-awareness Self-management	1.1 Self-Understanding 1.7 Cognitive and Affective Growth 3.3 Talent Development 4.1 Personal Competence	W.4
Lesson 17: Failure Isn't the End (p. 79)	Self-awareness Self-management	1.4 Awareness of Needs 3.2 Talent Development 3.5 Culturally Relevant Curriculum 4.1 Personal Competence 4.3 Leadership	W.6 W.7 W.8 W.9 L.6
Lesson 18: Responsible Or Not (p. 82)	Responsible decision-making	1.2 Self-Understanding 1.3 Self-Understanding 4.3 Leadership	W.2 L.6
Lesson 19: The Art of Making Decisions (p. 85)	Responsible decision-making	3.4 Instructional Strategies 4.5 Communication Competence	W.2 SL.5
Lesson 20: Let's Relax (p. 89)	Self-management	4.1 Personal Competence 4.3 Leadership	W.7 SL.1
Lesson 21: Overloaded (p. 92)	Self-management Relationship skills Responsible decision-making	1.1 Self-Understanding 1.2 Self-Understanding 4.1 Personal Competence	SL.1 SL.6 L.6
Lesson 22: This Is Stressing Me Out! (p. 95)	Self-management	1.1 Self-Understanding 4.1 Personal Competence	W.3 W.7 W.9
Lesson 23: A Stroll Through My Stress (p. 98)	Self-awareness Self-management	1.1 Self-Understanding 1.3 Self-Understanding 4.1 Personal Competence	W.4 W.7 W.9
Lesson 24: All About Balance (p. 102)	Self-management Responsible decision-making	4.1 Personal Competence 4.5 Communication Competence	SL.1 SL.4 SL.5
Unit IV			
Lesson 25: New Perspectives (p. 109)	Social-awareness	3.2 Talent Development 4.1 Personal Competence 4.5 Communication Competence	SL.1 SL.3 SL.6
Lesson 26: 101 Roads (p. 111)	Self-management Social-awareness	1.8 Cognitive and Affective Growth 3.4 Instructional Strategies 4.1 Personal Competence 4.2 Social Competence	SL.4 SL.5 SL.6
Lesson 27: The Art of Gratitude (p. 114)	Self-awareness Social-awareness	4.1 Personal Competence 4.2 Social Competence	W.3 W.4
Lesson 28: Me and My Friends (p. 116)	Social-awareness Relationship skills	4.1 Personal Competence 4.2 Social Competence	W.3 SL.1 SL.6

Table 1 Continued

LESSON	SEL COMPETENCY	NAGC STANDARDS	CCSS STANDARDS
Lesson 29: Don't Assume (p. 119)	Relationship skills Responsible decision-making	4.1 Personal Competence 4.2 Social Competence 4.5 Communication Competence	SL.3 SL.4
Lesson 30: My Cheer Squad (p. 122)	Relationship skills	4.1 Personal Competence 4.2 Social Competence	W.4 SL.1
Lesson 31: Do You Understand Me? (p. 126)	Relationship skills Responsible decision-making	4.2 Social Competence 4.5 Communication Competence	SL.1 SL.3 SL.4 SL.6
Lesson 32: Communication Roadblocks (p. 128)	Self-awareness Relationship skills Responsible decision-making	4.2 Social Competence 4.5 Communication Competence	SL.1 SL.3 SL.4 SL.6
Lesson 33: Learn to Listen (p. 130)	Relationship skills Responsible decision-making	4.2 Social Competence 4.5 Communication Competence	SL.1 SL.2 SL.3
Lesson 34: Attributes of a Leader (p. 133)	Social-awareness Responsible decision-making	4.3 Leadership 4.4 Cultural Competence	W.4 SL.1 SL.4 L.6
Lesson 35: The Sum of Its Parts (p. 135)	Social-awareness Relationship skills Responsible decision-making	4.2 Social Competence 4.4 Cultural Competence 4.5 Communication Competence	SL.1 SL.3 SL.4
Unit V			
Lesson 36: Many Ways to Learn (p. 141)	Self-awareness Self-management	1.2 Self-Understanding 1.7 Cognitive and Affective Growth 1.8 Cognitive and Affective Growth	W.7 W.8 W.9
Lesson 37: My Character and Qualities Inventory (p. 145)	Self-awareness Self-management	1.7 Cognitive and Affective Growth 1.8 Cognitive and Affective Growth 4.1 Personal Competence	W.7 W.8 W.9
Lesson 38: Divergence (p. 149)	Responsible decision-making	3.4 Instructional Strategies 4.5 Communication Competence	SL.3 SL.6
Lesson 39: Do What You Love (p. 152)	Responsible decision-making	1.8 Cognitive and Affective Growth 3.3 Talent Development 4.5 Communication Competence 5.7 Career Pathways	W.4 W.6
Lesson 40: I Am Enough (p. 155)	Self-awareness	1.2 Self-understanding 3.5 Culturally Relevant Curriculum 4.3 Leadership	SL.1 SL.3 SL.6
Lesson 41: Strengthening My Weaknesses (p. 160)	Self-management Social-awareness	1.1 Self-understanding 1.2 Self-understanding 1.6 Cognitive and Affective Growth	SL.1
Lesson 42: Plan Ahead (p. 163)	Self-management	4.5 Communication Competence 5.7 Career Pathways	W.4 L.6

Table 1 Continued

LESSON	SEL COMPETENCY	NAGC STANDARDS	CCSS STANDARDS
Lesson 43: So Many Choices (p. 166)	Self-management	1.8 Cognitive and Affective Growth 4.5 Communication Competence	W.7 W.8
Lesson 44: My Path (p. 171)	Self-management	3.3 Talent Development 3.4 Instructional Strategies 5.7 Career Pathways	W.7 W.8
Lesson 45: Mission Possible (p. 176)	Self-awareness Self-management	4.5 Communication Competence 5.7 Career Pathways	W.4 SL.6

Note. All Common Core State Standards listed correlate to the CCSS English Language Arts-Literacy K–12 College and Career Readiness Anchor standards.
Key: W = Writing; SL = Speaking & Listening; L = Language.

Section II
Social-Emotional Curriculum for Guiding Gifted Students

CHAPTER 5

Unit I
So I'm Gifted . . . What Does That Mean?

Defining giftedness is difficult for researchers, let alone laypeople or children. Most definitions start with intelligence and high potentiality. But that is not and cannot be the end of the story (Hébert, 2011). Researchers have expanded their view of giftedness in an effort to encapsulate the complexities of giftedness. Using theories that include Dabrowski's theory of emotional development and overexciteabilities, Gardner's ideas of multiple intelligences, and the more contemporary ideas of Sternberg's theory of wisdom and Renzulli's social capital, researchers now view giftedness as a collection of traits that change and develop over time (Hébert, 2011). These changes have made it even more difficult to explain giftedness to children. Nevertheless, Unit I attempts to do just that—provide a foundation of self-understanding for gifted children to begin their road of self-actualization.

"Giftedness isn't something you choose." This quote, Success Secret #1 from *101 Success Secrets for Gifted Kids*, sums up the major theme of this unit (Fonseca, 2011a, p. 8). Giftedness isn't something that a person chooses. It is a something a person *is*. It refers to the way a person thinks, feels, and interacts with the world. It changes over time. Evolves. But it doesn't become something else entirely. It simply becomes *more.* That is, when the gifted individual's talents are nurtured, when the emotional and social development is enriched, and when gifted students are appropriately engaged in meaningful opportunities to learn and grow, they are able to harness their gifts in more meaningful ways (Siegle, 2013).

Current research indicates that gifted children benefit from increased opportunities to understand their giftedness and talents, identify needs, and have opportunities to learn from appropriate role models (Ford, Tyson, Howard, & Harris, 2000; Grantham, 2004; Kong, 2013; Moon, 2009; Reis & Renzulli, 2004; Renzulli, 2009). The lessons in this unit are designed to allow gifted children to embrace everything it means to be gifted in the hopes that this increased awareness will enable and increase self-advocacy as gifted children begin their journey into secondary education.

LESSON OVERVIEW

There are only four lessons in this unit, each focused on an aspect of self-discovery including:

- self-awareness;
- expectations, real and perceived;
- identifying needs; and
- developing personal identity.

As you can see, the list is hardly exhaustive. It is meant only as a starting point for students, providing a foundation of knowledge that will shape and direct future lessons.

As I discussed in Chapter 4, it's important to create a safe and trusting environment for these and other lessons. The discussions that follow each activity have the potential to be very dynamic. This is more likely to happen when students develop trust. Focus on the guiding principles for each lesson, and weave your own authenticity into each activity.

EXTENSION OPPORTUNITIES

From the beginning I knew that I would not be able to offer many longer assignments due to the nature of these mini-lessons. However, I wanted to include a few additional activities that teachers could develop into opportunities for deeper exploration for students. In this unit, these can include the following:

- Write an autobiography.
- Read a biography and create a vlog or lesson highlighting the life of a well-known gifted individual (this can be tailored to student interest areas).
- Develop a mentorship program with younger students.

LESSON 1
THE MEANING OF GIFTEDNESS

OBJECTIVE

By the end of the lesson, students will be able to:

▓ understand the full definition of giftedness and how it specifically applies to them, and

▓ recognize some of the myths and assumptions about giftedness.

GUIDING QUESTIONS FOR STUDENTS

▓ What does it mean to be gifted?

▓ How am I different from my typical peers?

▓ What are the myths and assumptions about giftedness? Has anyone ever made those assumptions about me?

GUIDING PRINCIPLES

Giftedness is hardwired and involves a specific collection of traits that include cognition, personality, and emotional characteristics. There are many prevailing myths and assumptions about giftedness held by teachers, friends, and family. Some of these include the idea that gifted individuals are good at everything and don't need support in the school setting. It is important for gifted children to understand the characteristics of giftedness, as well as some of the assumptions others may have about them in order to make the most of their gifts and potential.

MATERIALS

▓ Handout 1.1: Gifts

▓ Handout 1.2: Myths and Assumptions

▓ Crayons, colored pencils, or other writing utensils for students

▓ Whiteboard, flipchart, or smart board for discussion

INTRODUCTION

Introduce guiding principles and the Gifts worksheet. Give each student a large piece of paper and an assortment of art supplies. Have each student write his or her name in the center of the page.

ACTIVITY

- As a group, discuss the common traits of giftedness in the areas of thinking (cognition), feeling (emotions), and behavior (personality). Ask each student to brainstorm a list of traits for each section to share with the whole group. Instruct students to write these in the chart on Handout 1.1 after the brainstorming session.
- Using the large paper and art supplies, ask the students to create a word cloud of the traits most representative of themselves. (Note: This activity can also be done on a computer and printed out.)
- Pass out the Myths and Assumptions handout. Ask students to circle the assumptions people have made about them.

DISCUSSION

Ask students to share their word clouds. Discuss the assumptions some people make about gifted children and why they can happen. Use the following discussion questions to aid the conversation:

- Which traits of giftedness do you enjoy the most? Which are the most problematic?
- What is the biggest assumption that people make about your giftedness?
- What would you like to say to people about these assumptions?

ASSESSMENT

Using the word clouds and assumptions worksheet, instruct the students to write a 1–2 sentence tagline for one aspect of giftedness. Evaluate the students' responses based on appropriate standards.

Name: _____ Date: _____

GIFTS

Directions: Brainstorm a list of traits for each section. Be sure to answer the questions below.

TYPICAL TRAITS

THINKING	FEELING	BEHAVIOR

Which three "Thinking" traits do you exhibit?

1. _____

2. _____

3. _____

Which three "Feeling" traits do you exhibit?

1. _____

2. _____

3. _____

Which three "Behavior" traits do you exhibit?

1. _____

2. _____

3. _____

MYTHS AND ASSUMPTIONS

Directions: Take a moment and read each assumption. Check those assumptions people have thought about you, as well as the assumptions you may have had about yourself.

	There's no such thing as gifted.		All kids are gifted in some way.	
	Gifted children are good at everything.		This should be easy for you—you're "gifted."	
	Gifted people are nerds.		Everything comes easily to a gifted person.	
	Gifted kids who skipped grades are too immature.		Gifted people shouldn't complain—everything comes easy for them.	
	Gifted kids don't need extra help.		I wouldn't want to be gifted—that means you're weird.	
	Gifted kids don't need to study.		Gifted kids can get into any college they want.	
	If a gifted person does poorly on a test, it means they aren't really gifted.		Some kids outgrow their giftedness.	
	You are either smart or you aren't.		You either have talents in an area or you don't.	

Now, take a moment and write a few words or sentences to describe what being gifted means for you. What do you want people to know about you?

_____

_____

_____

_____

_____

_____

LESSON 2
NOT JUST GIFTED

OBJECTIVE

By the end of the lesson, students will be able to:

- understand the full definition of giftedness and how it specifically applies to them,
- be able to analyze the pros and cons of giftedness traits, and
- identify any specific needs they have.

GUIDING QUESTION FOR STUDENTS

- What are my interests, strengths, and needs as a gifted student?

GUIDING PRINCIPLES

Giftedness is often widely misunderstood. Most people understand a gifted individual as related to performance in academic endeavors. However, giftedness involves more than simple performance in school. Giftedness refers to how a person thinks, sees, and interacts with other people and the world around him or her.

MATERIALS

- Handout 2.1: T-shirt cutout
- Crayons, colored pencils, or other writing utensils for students
- Whiteboard, flipchart, or smart board for discussion

INTRODUCTION

Introduce guiding principles and vocabulary. Give each student a large T-shirt cutout (Handout 2.1). Have students write their names in the center of the shirt.

ACTIVITY

- Instruct students to write one or two words about their interests, their strengths, and their giftedness traits on their shirts. Use different colors for interests, strengths, and traits.
- Instruct students to write the more difficult or negative aspects of being gifted on their shirts in a different color.

- Ask students to share their T-shirts with their table groups, pointing out an interest, a strength, and something they view as negative.
- Ask students to brainstorm ways to turn negative traits into positive traits. Are any specific needs discovered through the brainstorming? Ask students to write their needs on the T-shirt in a new color.

DISCUSSION

As a group, discuss how giftedness means different things to different people. Discuss the pros and cons of giftedness as well as any needs some gifted individuals may have. Use the following discussion questions to aid the conversation:

- How do you show your giftedness?
- Are there areas you are concerned about? What are they?
- What are your specific needs? How can they be met?

ASSESSMENT

Instruct students to write a letter, create a class blog post, or write a short blog explaining giftedness and what needs a gifted person may have in a traditional classroom. Include ways that teachers and educators can meet the needs of gifted students within the context of school. Evaluate the students' projects based on appropriate standards.

T-SHIRT CUTOUT

LESSON 3
GREAT EXPECTATIONS

OBJECTIVE

By the end of the lesson, students will be able to:

- understand the expectations they place on themselves,
- understand the expectations placed on them by others, and
- manage their emotions and maintain balance.

GUIDING QUESTIONS FOR STUDENTS

- What are the expectations that I have for myself?
- What are the expectations that my teachers and parents have for me?
- How are these expectations influenced by my giftedness?

GUIDING PRINCIPLES

Gifted children often have many expectations about their academic performance. Many times these expectations are unrealistic. Additionally, teachers and parents have expectations for these children. It is important for gifted children to learn how to discern between appropriate expectations and unrealistic perfectionism.

MATERIALS

- Handout 3.1: Expectations
- Balloons
- Markers, pencils
- Whiteboard, flipchart, or smart board for discussion

INTRODUCTION

Introduce guiding principles to students. Give each student a balloon, a marker, and the Expectations worksheet (Handout 3.1).

ACTIVITY

- Instruct students to blow up the balloons and tie them off. Assist students as necessary.

- Ask students to name expectations that their parents have, teachers have, or they have for themselves. Ask the students to write the expectations all over their balloons. Be careful not to press too hard and pop the balloon.
- Using the Expectations worksheet, complete the top portion listing expectations held by teachers, parents, or family members and the students. Discuss the various ways these expectations make the students feel.
- Write down the feeling words on the balloons next to the expectations.
- Discuss how to discern realistic from unrealistic expectations. Discuss the importance of developing realistic expectations.
- Ask the students to carefully pop the balloons. Tell the students: "You now have a clean slate. No preconceived expectations. How do you feel now?"
- Using the Expectations worksheet, complete the bottom section listing realistic expectations.

DISCUSSION

As a group, discuss the importance of maintaining realistic expectations. Use the following discussion questions to guide the conversation:

- Do your parents have unrealistic expectations for you? How do you know this?
- Do you have unrealistic expectations for yourself? How do you know this?
- How do the unrealistic expectations make you feel?
- How can you make sure your expectations are realistic?

ASSESSMENT

Instruct students to write a letter or poem to a teacher or parent or create a short vlog stating the importance of holding realistic expectations. Evaluate students' projects based on appropriate standards.

EXPECTATIONS

SECTION 1

Directions: Complete the worksheet with expectations you've experienced.

EXPECTATIONS MY FRIENDS AND FAMILY HAVE FOR ME	EXPECTATIONS MY SCHOOL/ TEACHERS HAVE FOR ME	EXPECTATIONS I HAVE FOR MYSELF

SECTION 2

Directions: Take 3–5 of the expectations from the above list and rewrite them, making sure they are realistic.

_____

_____

_____

_____

_____

_____

_____

_____

_____

LESSON 4
THE STORY OF MY LIFE

OBJECTIVE

By the end of the lesson, students will be able to:

- understand the full definition of giftedness and how it specifically applies to them,
- be able to analyze the pros and cons of giftedness traits, and
- identify any specific needs they have.

GUIDING QUESTIONS FOR STUDENTS

- What are my talents, interests, and strengths as a gifted student? How do I want to apply them to future aspirations?

GUIDING PRINCIPLES

Gifted children benefit from talent development at a young age. It is not enough to assume their gifts will lead to a fulfilling future. Some people assume that giftedness automatically means success as an adult. However, research indicates that talent development throughout a gifted child's life will lead to a more fulfilling future.

MATERIALS

- Crayons, colored pencils, or other writing utensils for students
- Old magazines, scissors, glue
- Whiteboard, flipchart, or smart board for discussion

INTRODUCTION

Introduce guiding principles. Give old magazines, art supplies, and a blank piece of paper to students.

ACTIVITY

- As a group, brainstorm different careers and lifestyles that the students find interesting. Use the magazines for inspiration.
- Instruct students to cut out pictures that represent the lifestyle they would like to enjoy as an adult.

■ Ask students to brainstorm ideas of their future life as an adult. Students may work in groups; however, each student must develop his or her own life story.

■ Instruct students to either compose an essay, creative video, or blog, or create a graphic design that expresses their future career and lifestyle choices.

DISCUSSION

As a large group, discuss the benefits of having goals to reach your long-term objectives. Discuss how giftedness and talents influence career choices. Use the following discussion questions to aid the conversation:

■ Why is it important to enjoy what you would do as a career?

■ Do you think it is important to consider skills, interests, financial potential, or other factors when deciding on career goals?

■ Are there different ways people can achieve their goals? How can a person choose the path that is best for him or her?

ASSESSMENT

Evaluate the students' projects based on appropriate standards.

CHAPTER 6

Unit II
Don't Forget About Emotional Intelligence

Emotional intelligence has been center of much research as educators begin to understand the social-emotional aspects of achievement (CASEL, n.d.; Lee & Olszewski-Kubilius, 2006). Skills, including self-awareness, understanding and managing emotions, social skills, and conflict resolution, are increasingly valued as research continues to demonstrate the need for these skills in the classroom (CASEL, 2005). These skills also overlap with many of the prevailing theories surrounding gifted development. Indeed, many of the components of emotional intelligence overlap with theories of talent development, personal and identity development, and social-cognitive theory (Moon, 2009). These theories provide the framework for the development of an affective curriculum.

The purpose of this unit is to enhance many of the basic skills within emotional intelligence. In truth, the following sections capitalize on those skills as well. Using strategies from cognitive-behavioral theory and positive psychology, these lessons were developed to increase social-emotional compentencies in self-awareness, self-management, and social competency.

UNIT OVERVIEW

The nine lessons in this unit cover three broad skill areas as follows:
- *Self-awareness* (Lessons 5–7): These lessons focus on the idea of increasing self-awareness through self-evaluation, recognizing emotions, and mindfulness.
- *Managing emotions* (Lessons 8–10): These lessons involve understanding emotions, perspective taking, and developing emotional awareness and balance.

> ▣ *Conflict resolution* (Lessons 11–13): Conflict resolution, anger management, and problem solving are discussed through these lessons.

To increase the value to gifted children, each lesson can include increased cultural diversity as appropriate for your group. Also, supporting the lessons with additional readings will deepen the content you provide for your students. Use the discussions to allow for a deeper, personal exploration of discussion topics.

EXTENSION OPPORTUNITIES

Some potential extension activities that can build on the lessons in this unit include the following:

- ▣ Extended journaling.
- ▣ Research different cultures related to interest areas and create mini-lessons about that culture.
- ▣ Music and art exploration.
- ▣ Service project involvement.
- ▣ Develop a public service announcement (PSA) about one of the concepts.

LESSON 5
SOARING WITH STRENGTHS

OBJECTIVE

By the end of the lesson, students will be able to:
- identify personal strengths.

GUIDING QUESTION FOR THE STUDENTS

- What are my personal strengths?

GUIDING PRINCIPLES

Many gifted children have difficulties recognizing their strengths. Caught in a wave of perfectionism, gifted children tend to overfocus on weaknesses and ignore their strengths. It's important for children to learn to identify strengths and weaknesses correctly, and review positive traits during times of difficulty. (*Note.* Lesson #41 (p. 160), "Strengthening My Weaknesses," will provide an opportunity to develop strategies to address personal weaknesses. Educators may want to use this lesson in tandem with Lesson #41.)

MATERIALS

- Handout 5.1: My Strengths
- Handout 5.2: Bird Silhouette Cutout
- Crayons, colored pencils, or other writing utensils for students

INTRODUCTION

Introduce guiding principles and any required vocabulary. Give each student several bird cutouts and the My Strengths worksheet.

ACTIVITY

- As a whole group, discuss the meanings of strengths and weaknesses, focusing on the importance of recognizing both.
- Ask students to brainstorm a list of their personal strengths. These should be written on Handout 5.1.
- Working in dyads, ask students to review their lists to see if there are additional strengths that can be added.

■ Ask students to write down their strengths on the bird cutouts. Decorate the birds. The birds can be displayed in the room on a tree or similar board or hung from the ceiling.

DISCUSSION

As a group, discuss the importance of identifying strengths and weaknesses. Include a discussion of how gifted individuals may struggle with the task and why. Use the following discussion questions to aid the conversation:

■ Was it difficult isolating personal strengths?
■ What are some ways you can remember your strengths when you get stuck or experience frustration?
■ Why is it important to clarify your understanding of your personal strengths?

ASSESSMENT

Evaluate the students' responses based on appropriate standards.

Name:_____ Date: _____

MY STRENGTHS

Directions: Brainstorm lists of your strengths and write each in the appropriate column.

QUALITIES I SEE AS MY STRENGTHS	THINGS TEACHERS HAVE SAID ARE MY STRENGTHS	THINGS MY FAMILY AND FRIENDS HAVE SAID ARE MY STRENGTHS

BIRD SILHOUETTE CUTOUT

LESSON 6
AM I AFRAID?

OBJECTIVE

By the end of the lesson, students will be able to:

- develop a personal definition of fear,
- identify and recognize personal fear triggers, and
- develop coping strategies.

GUIDING QUESTIONS FOR STUDENTS

- When am I afraid?
- What does fear look like to me?
- What can I do to stop being afraid?

GUIDING PRINCIPLES

Gifted individuals often experience intense emotions, including fear. Learning to recognize how fear impacts you as well as learning how to reduce the influence of fear on your behavior is important in order to develop appropriate risk-taking skills.

MATERIALS

- Handout 6.1: Am I Afraid?
- Whiteboard, flipchart, or smart board for discussion
- Space for each group to demonstrate skits

INTRODUCTION

Arrange the desks into small table groups of 2–4 students. Introduce guiding principles and any vocabulary needed.

ACTIVITY

- As a group, discuss what fear is and is not. Ask each student to write down a benefit of fear, and a drawback of being afraid. Ask the students to discuss benefits and drawbacks within their table groups.
- As a group, discuss the common symptoms—physical, emotional, and behavioral—of fear. Ask each table group to brainstorm its own list of fear symptoms.

- Ask table groups to brainstorm a list of events or situations that trigger fear response. Share the lists as a whole group.
- Give each table group Handout 6.1: Am I Afraid? Each table group will now develop a short skit to demonstrate a fear trigger and a typical reaction. A second table group will observe this skit and strategize ways to avoid the fear trigger or reduce the negative impact.
- Rotate which table group performs the skit and which table group observes until all groups have had an opportunity to do both.

DISCUSSION

Discuss how fear can be both a benefit and a drawback. Discuss common fear triggers and how fear manifests in gifted individuals. The following questions can help guide the conversation:

- What does fear mean to you?
- When do you know that you are afraid?
- What kinds of strategies can you use to reduce the negative impact of fear?

ASSESSMENT

Evaluate the students' skits and responses based on appropriate standards.

AM I AFRAID?

Directions: As a group, indicate what fear trigger and symptoms you will use in your skit. Write these down in the appropriate boxes. In the last box, write 1–3 strategies to handle the fear you are demonstrating. Compare these again to the ones the other groups develop and add to your list if needed.

FEAR TRIGGER

FEAR SYMPTOMS

CALMING STRATEGIES

LESSON 7
BEING MINDFUL

OBJECTIVE

By the end of the lesson, students will be able to:

- define the concepts of mindfulness and flow,
- provide examples of mindfulness, and
- explain how mindfulness relates to emotional development.

GUIDING QUESTIONS FOR STUDENTS

- Why is it important to live in the moment?
- How can I bring mindfulness into my life?

GUIDING PRINCIPLES

We live in a noisy, busy world. At times, it's hard to hear ourselves think. Trapped in the monotony of the mundane, it is easy to lose track of our own authentic thoughts, hopes, and desires. This lack of focus and clarity can prevent us from reaching our goals in life. The impact is magnified for gifted students who frequently live life in a deeply intense manner. Learning the art of being mindful is one way to redevelop the ability to focus and learn how to live in the moment. Furthermore, mindfulness can lead to something called "flow"—that moment of heightened focus when productivity is at its highest. Creating a daily habit of mindfulness can cultivate increased periods of "flow" for children and adults.

MATERIALS

- Handout 7.1: Mindfulness Reflection
- A bell
- Snacks
- Crayons, colored pencils, or other writing utensils for students
- Whiteboard, flipchart, or smart board for discussion

INTRODUCTION

Arrange desks in groups of 3–6. Provide each student with a snack. Introduce guiding principles and required vocabulary.

ACTIVITY

- Explain to students that you will be practicing a lesson in mindfulness. For the next 5 minutes, the students will do nothing but eat their snack. Set a calm and relaxing tone in the classroom.
- Instruct students to clear their thoughts and focus only on eating the snack. Ask them to pay attention to their senses—how does the food taste? How does it smell or feel when being eaten? Remind students that there is no talking. It is only a period of focused eating. Encourage students to chew each bite 15 times and count them. Nothing else. Ring a bell to indicate the start of the "mindfulness" activity.
- In 5 minutes, ring the bell indicating the end of the session. Pass out the reflection worksheet (Handout 7.1) and ask students to take a moment to reflect on the eating exercise. Ask them to write their thoughts on the worksheet.

DISCUSSION

As a group, discuss mindfulness and the eating activity. Use the following discussion questions to aid the conversation:

- Was it easy to focus only on eating for 5 minutes?
- If it was difficult, what made it difficult?
- What are some other activities in which mindfulness can be included?
- How can being mindful lead to periods of flow?

ASSESSMENT

Evaluate the students' discussions based on appropriate standards. (*Note.* As an extension, add a mindfulness journal and ask students to practice mindfulness for 5 minutes daily. Alternatively, ask students to incorporate a period of mindfulness into their daily routine and reflect on their experiences in a journal.)

MINDFULNESS REFLECTION

Directions: Complete the questions after your activity.

1. Was this easy or hard for you to do?

_____

_____

_____

_____

_____

_____

2. Did you experience some difficulty or discomfort? Why do you think you felt this way?

_____

_____

_____

_____

_____

3. Would you want to find time to be mindful more often? Why or why not?

_____

_____

_____

_____

_____

_____

LESSON 8
UNDERSTANDING EMOTIONS

OBJECTIVE

By the end of the lesson, students will be able to:
- identify a variety of emotional states, and
- recognize personal emotional responses.

GUIDING QUESTIONS FOR STUDENTS

- What types of emotions do I experience throughout the day and why?
- How intense are my emotions?

GUIDING PRINCIPLES

Many gifted individuals experience intense emotions throughout the day. However, it is not always easy to identify these emotions or their triggers. Learning about a variety of emotional responses, as well as how they are triggered, is necessary in order to develop emotional management skills.

MATERIALS

- Handout 8.1: Understanding Emotions
- Art supplies to create a graphic
- Crayons, colored pencils, or other writing utensils for students
- Whiteboard, flipchart, or smart board for discussion

INTRODUCTION

Introduce guiding principles and any required vocabulary. Provide Handout 8.1 to each student.

ACTIVITY

- Explain what emotions are and review some of the basic emotional states. Invite students to brainstorm additional emotions and describe them in terms of positive or negative emotions and what may trigger them. Consider everything from social interactions, to music or art, to physical pain, etc.
- Ask students to complete Section 1 of the worksheet.

▨ Instruct students to think of 2–3 events that elicited an emotional response. Using these events, ask students to complete Section 2 of the worksheet.

▨ Based on this information, ask students to make a visual representation of one emotional reaction.

DISCUSSION

Discuss the value in understanding emotions. Include a discussion of gifted children and intense emotions. Use the following discussion questions to aid the conversation:

▨ Do you think you react more intensely than others? In what way?

▨ What is the value in understanding emotions and their triggers?

▨ Are you comfortable with your emotional reactions?

ASSESSMENT

Evaluate the students' spoken and visual responses based on appropriate standards.

Name:_____ Date: _____

UNDERSTANDING EMOTIONS

SECTION 1

Directions: Complete the table based on the group discussion.

EMOTION	MENTAL, PHYSICAL, OR BEHAVIORAL REACTION	POSSIBLE TRIGGER
Sadness	I feel down, depressed. Slumped shoulders, crying.	Someone hurt my feelings.

SECTION 2

Directions: Complete the table based on personal experiences.

EVENT (PERSONAL)	REACTION (PHYSICAL, MENTAL, OR EMOTIONAL)	EMOTION DEMONSTRATED
My teacher asked me to rewrite an essay for a better grade.	I came home and screamed at my mom, saying the teacher was mean. I cried afterward and felt bad about what I had said.	Frustration, anger, and maybe disappointment that I hadn't done well on the task.
1.		
2.		
3.		

LESSON 9
MY EMOTIONAL VOCABULARY

OBJECTIVE

By the end of the lesson, students will be able to:
- identify a variety of emotional states,
- define various emotional states for themselves, and
- develop a personal emotional vocabulary.

GUIDING QUESTIONS FOR STUDENTS

- What am I feeling?
- How do I describe my emotional states?

GUIDING PRINCIPLES

Gifted individuals often express significant emotional intensity. This intensity can be hard to manage, partly due to the individual's inability to clearly define the emotions and express when he or she is feeling overwhelmed. Learning how to talk about emotions, as well as how to clearly express a variety of emotional states, can give gifted individuals the distance needed to begin to control and reset their internal emotional states.

MATERIALS

- Handout 9.1: My Emotions
- 3 x 5 index cards, hole punch, string
- Crayons, colored pencils, or other writing utensils for students
- Whiteboard, flipchart, or smart board for discussion

INTRODUCTION

Set up tables in groups of 2–4. Introduce guiding principles and vocabulary. Give each student Handout 9.1, 5–10 index cards, string, and art supplies.

ACTIVITY

- Discuss the basic emotional states of joy, sadness, love, and anger. Discuss additional emotional states that are similar to the four listed. Ask students to brainstorm a list of emotional adjectives.

- Working in small groups, discuss what various emotional states "look" like.
- Ask students to complete the My Emotions worksheet, leaving the last two questions blank. Students can work in groups, but the worksheets must reflect each student's personal emotions and descriptions.
- Have students choose five emotions for the index cards. Ask students to write the emotion on one side, and put a description and picture (face or symbol) on the other side. Join cards together with string to make a ring of emotion cards.
- Have students complete the last two questions of the worksheet.

DISCUSSION

Discuss the importance of developing an emotional vocabulary, especially for gifted individuals. Use the following discussion questions to aid the conversation:

- How do you discuss your feelings?
- What would be the advantage of developing an emotional vocabulary?
- What is the advantage of being able to express your emotions verbally, not just through your actions?

ASSESSMENT

Evaluate the students' projects based on appropriate standards.

MY EMOTIONS

SECTION 1

Directions: Complete the table based on the group discussion.

EMOTION	WHAT IT LOOKS LIKE
FRustRation	Clenched fists, tight jaw, shallow bReathing

SECTION 2

Directions: Answer the following questions when you are finished with your emotions ring.

1. Why is it important to identify different types of emotions?

   _____

   _____

   _____

2. Why did you choose the emotions you used in your ring?

   _____

   _____

   _____

LESSON 10
MY HULA HOOP

OBJECTIVE

By the end of the lesson, students will be able to:

- explain how to achieve emotional balance, and
- identify strategies to increase emotional control.

GUIDING QUESTIONS FOR STUDENTS

- How can I stay in control of my emotions?
- How do I demonstrate increased self-management skills when I am upset or frustrated?

GUIDING PRINCIPLES

Sometimes life can be overwhelming. It can feel as though we are victims to our own emotions and the world around us. Managing our emotional responses during these periods of overwhelm can be difficult. However, learning to mange emotions and maintain a positive perspective is a vital skill toward the development of emotional intelligence. Learning to take responsibility for your emotions and regulate your emotional reactions are all aspects of developing self-management skills.

MATERIALS

- Handout 10.1: My Hula Hoop Graphic Organizer
- Crayons, colored pencils, or other writing utensils for students
- Whiteboard, flipchart, or smart board for discussion

INTRODUCTION

Introduce guiding principles and any required vocabulary. Give each student the handout.

ACTIVITY

- Ask students to think about a time when they felt overwhelmed. What happened? How did they feel? Share several examples.
- Instruct the students to make a list of the overwhelming events in Section 1 of the graphic organizer. For each item listed, ask students to determine if they

had control over the event or not. Ask students to list their typical reactions and determine which reactions were under their control and which were not.

- Direct students to Section 2 of the worksheet. Ask them to complete the graphic, listing only those events within their control inside the circle, and everything else outside of the circle. Ask students to add their reactions to the graphic in a different color.

DISCUSSION

As a group, discuss the results of the exercise. Use the following discussion questions to aid the conversation:

- How many events were completely within your control? How many were not?
- How many reactions were within your control? How many were not?
- What conclusions can be drawn from this activity?

ASSESSMENT

Instruct students to write a short paragraph explaining the findings of the activity. Be sure they include what new information was gained and how they can use these findings. Evaluate the students' paragraphs based on appropriate standards.

MY HULA HOOP GRAPHIC ORGANIZER

SECTION 1

Directions: Complete the table based on the group discussion.

OVERWHELMING EVENT	PERSONAL CONTROL Y/N

SECTION 2

Directions: List events within your control inside the circle. List events outside your control outside the circle.

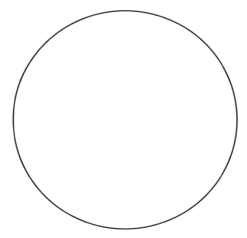

LESSON 11
UNDERSTANDING TRIGGERS

OBJECTIVE

By the end of the lesson, students will be able to:

- identify situations or actions that trigger a strong emotional response,
- determine the intensity of their emotions, and
- identify 1–2 coping responses.

GUIDING QUESTION FOR STUDENTS

- What situations are most likely to trigger a strong emotional reaction from me like frustration or anger?

GUIDING PRINCIPLES

Gifted individuals often experience strong emotional reactions to people and situations related to emotional overexciteability. Sometimes these emotions can overwhelm gifted individuals, inhibiting their coping mechanisms and escalating their reactions. It is important to learn what your personal triggers are in order to develop increased tolerance and emotional balance.

Identifying triggers, recognizing the intensity of your emotional response, and utilizing a coping strategy when needed are all necessary in order to achieve emotional balance.

MATERIALS

- Handout 11.1: Triggers Wheel
- Magazines, cutouts, and other graphic art supplies
- Crayons, colored pencils, or other writing utensils for students
- Whiteboard, flipchart, or smart board for discussion

INTRODUCTION

Arrange desks in groups of 2–4. Introduce guiding principles and any necessary vocabulary. Give each student the handout and a variety or art supplies.

ACTIVITY

- Discuss what it means to be emotionally triggered. Brainstorm the kinds of events or situations that would result in a negative response.
- Have each student write the things that trigger him or her in the inner section of the "wheel."
- Discuss the different types of emotions that occur when there is a negative response. Instruct students to write these emotions in the middle section of the wheel.
- Discuss coping strategies children can use when experiencing negative emotions. Focusing on at least one triggering event, ask groups to brainstorm coping strategies. Instruct students to write these in the outer sections of the wheel.
- If time permits, students may decorate their wheels.

DISCUSSION

Discuss the temporal nature of triggers. Ask students to brainstorm ways to reduce the impact of their triggers on their emotional reactions. Use the following discussion questions to aid the conversation:

- How are triggers changed or reduced over time?
- What are some ways to change the effect a trigger has on you?
- If you are triggered into an angry or frustrated response, what can you do to reduce the intensity of your response?

ASSESSMENT

Evaluate the students' projects based on appropriate standards.

Name: _____ Date: _____

TRIGGERS WHEEL

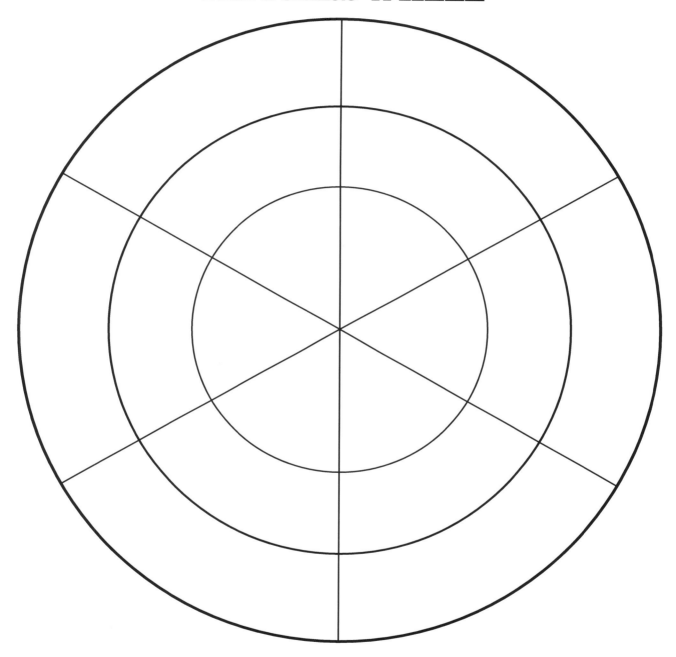

LESSON 12
HOW MAD AM I?

OBJECTIVE

By the end of the lesson, students will be able to:

- understand how they express anger,
- identify the things that elicit anger, and
- explain ways to reduce anger.

GUIDING QUESTIONS FOR STUDENTS

- What things make me angry, and how do I currently respond to them?
- How should I respond?

GUIDING PRINCIPLES

Feeling upset or angry is a normal human reaction. However, aggressive responses to angry feelings are seldom appropriate. Learning to manage angry feelings is an important aspect of emotional intelligence and self-mastery.

MATERIALS

- Handout 12.1: How Mad Am I?
- Crayons, colored pencils, or other writing utensils for students
- Whiteboard, flipchart, or smart board for discussion

INTRODUCTION

Introduce guiding principles. Give students the handout.

ACTIVITY

- Discuss the difference between feeling anger and acting aggressively. Ask students for examples of things that make them angry, include everything from personal conflicts to bigger societal issues (if applicable).
- Instruct students to complete the worksheet, rating each presented scenario.
- Ask students to brainstorm possible ways to cool down when angry. Instruct students to write the strategies on the appropriate section of the worksheet.

DISCUSSION

As a group, discuss the importance of understanding anger and possible coping strategies. Use the following discussion questions to aid the conversation:

- What did you learn about your anger?
- What are some ways to reduce angry feelings?
- How can you remember to use these strategies when you are angry?

ASSESSMENT

Evaluate the students' responses based on appropriate standards.

Name:_____ Date: _____

HOW MAD AM I?

Directions: Complete the table based on the activity.

EVENT	HOW I REACT . . .	MY ANGER RATING: 1–5 (1 BEING LOWEST, 5 BEING HIGHEST)
I get a bad grade on a test		
My friend gets angry with me		
Global warming		
Society problems		
I lose my homework		
My sister yells at me		
My teammate messes up a play		
My family changes plans		

What kinds of events make me the angriest?

_____

_____

_____

How can I reduce my anger?

_____

_____

_____

LESSON 13
BEING A CREATIVE PROBLEM SOLVER

OBJECTIVE

By the end of the lesson, students will be able to:

- demonstrate creative problem solving skills, and
- explain why it is important to develop problem-solving skills.

GUIDING QUESTION FOR STUDENTS

- How can I creatively solve unusual problems?

GUIDING PRINCIPLES

Creative problem solving is an important skill, necessary as we tackle life's bigger problems. Learning to tackle problems from a creative, open-ended point of view can translate to creative problem solving with bigger world issues.

MATERIALS

- Handout 13.1: Solutions to Real-World Problems
- Large paper posted somewhere in the room
- Crayons, colored pencils, or other writing utensils for students
- Whiteboard, flipchart, or smart board for discussion

INTRODUCTION

Arrange tables into groups of 2–4. Introduce guiding principles.

ACTIVITY

- Instruct table groups to brainstorm answers to the question "What really bothers you?" Give initial examples for students to get them started. Possible examples include traffic jams, burning toast, slow computers, etc. The idea is to generate a list of real-world problems.
- Once the groups have generated lists, invite students to write their answers on a master list for the class. No item can be repeated.
- Instruct table groups to pick five "problems" and generate as many solutions to the problem as possible. Write the solutions on Handout 13.1 and share with the class.
- Instruct students to complete the questions at the end of the worksheet.

DISCUSSION

Discuss the importance of creating solutions to everyday problems. Use these discussion questions to aid the conversation:

- Was it easy to brainstorm solutions to the problem? Why or why not?
- What is something to consider when solving problems?
- If you were to tackle one of the problems, how would you begin to implement a solution?

ASSESSMENT

Instruct students to write a letter in which they explain their solution to a real-world problem. Be sure to include a plan for implementing the solution. Evaluate the students' responses based on appropriate standards.

SOLUTIONS TO REAL-WORLD PROBLEMS

PROBLEM	POTENTIAL SOLUTIONS

Pick one problem and solution. How would you begin to implement your solution? What things do you need to consider when solving the problem?

_____

_____

_____

_____

_____

CHAPTER 7

Unit III
Daily Habits for Successful Living

Identity development is often a complicated process, developing over time like other aspects of personality. With gifted individuals, the importance of supporting positive identity formation in middle childhood and later can be seen throughout the research (Hébert, 2011). However, supporting gifted children can be difficult, as the developmental trajectory of gifted children is often a complex and highly individual process (Cross, 2011; Peterson, 2009). Consideration of the individual child, as well as the incorporation of evidence-based strategies including discussion groups, journaling and self-reflection, and cultural diversity training can be powerful tools in addressing the needs of gifted children in this area (Day-Vines, Patton, Quek, & Wood, 2009; Ford, 2006; Neihart, 2002; Siegle, 2013).

The purpose of this unit is to support positive identify formation through the development of emotional intelligence, executive functioning, coping skills, and self-awareness (Siegle, 2013; VanTassel-Baska, 2009; Wilcox, 2013). As these skills are developed and enhanced, gifted children are more prepared to delve into the concepts of risk-taking and talent development in the upcoming chapters.

UNIT OVERVIEW

The 11 lessons in this unit cover four broad skill areas as follows:

- *Optimism and positive self-talk* (Lessons 14–16): These lessons focus on the idea of developing a positive regard for the future through the development of positive self-reflection, and developing a positive mindset.
- *Motivation and responsibility* (Lessons 17–18): These lessons involve positive perspective taking and the development of personal and social responsibility.

- *Decision-making skills* (Lesson 19): This lesson explores decision-making paradigms.
- *Stress management* (Lesson 20–24): These lessons focus on coping strategies including relaxation, self-evaluation, and developing healthy lifestyle habits.

It is vital that cultural diversity is woven through these lessons in order to enhance and support the needs of a culturally diverse population. Adding art and technology components beyond those within the lessons will also increase student engagement (Pyryt, 2003; VanTassel-Baska et al., 2009). To increase the value to gifted children, each lesson can include more cultural diversity as appropriate for your group. Also, supporting the lessons with additional readings will deepen the content you provide for your students. Use the discussions to allow for a deeper, personal exploration of discussion topics.

EXTENSION OPPORTUNITIES

Some potential extension activities that can build on the lessons in this unit include the following:

- Extended journaling.
- Bring experts into class for discussion/enrichment.
- Develop a coping skills newsletter or blog unit.
- Research the lives of gifted individuals who have experienced failure. Write a graphic novel or comic strip highlighting the positive outcomes of their "failure."

LESSON 14
THE PERSON IN THE MIRROR

OBJECTIVE

By the end of the lesson, students will be able to:

- identify personal strengths,
- understand the importance of focusing on strengths, and
- use strength areas as a tool to assist in maintaining emotional balance.

GUIDING QUESTIONS FOR STUDENTS

- What are my strengths?
- How can I use them to help me stay in balance?

GUIDING PRINCIPLES

Many gifted individuals struggle with self-confidence, often believing their "gifts" aren't really gifts. Imposter syndrome, as the lack of confidence is often called, happens when gifted individuals think their abilities and potential are nothing more than things their parents or teachers have said, but not a true evaluation of themselves. It is important for gifted individuals to recognize their many strengths, especially when they are overly frustrated or stressed.

MATERIALS

- Handout 14.1: My Strengths and Gifts Graphic Organizer
- Handout 14.2: Strengths Word Bank
- 3 x 5 cards, yarn, and other art supplies to decorate the cards
- Whiteboard, flipchart, or smart board for discussion

INTRODUCTION

Arrange the desks into groups of 2–4. Put cards and art supplies at each table group. Provide each student with a word bank and graphic organizer. Introduce guiding principles and any required vocabulary.

ACTIVITY

- Discuss the concept of self-confidence and imposter syndrome. Ask table groups to discuss ways they struggle with confidence, as well as areas of strong self-confidence.
- Ask students to complete the My Strengths graphic organizer, using the word banks for inspiration. Students can work in groups, but the organizers must reflect each student's personal experiences.
- Have students choose 5–10 strengths. If the students get stuck, ask them to work in pairs to help them see their strengths.
- On the front of an index card, ask the students to write a strength (1–2 words) in the center. On the back, ask students to write 1–2 sentences describing that strength.
- Decorate cards to reflect the student's personal style and interest.

DISCUSSION

Discuss the importance of recognizing individual strengths and positive self-talk. Use the following discussion questions to aid the conversation:

- Why is it harder to think of strengths instead of areas of difficulty?
- What are the benefits of a positive mindset?
- What can you do to maintain a positive outlook, even when things are difficult?

ASSESSMENT

Ask students to write a letter to their less confident selves. In the letter, they should highlight their strengths and how to navigate through difficult times. Evaluate the students' responses based on appropriate standards.

MY STRENGTHS AND GIFTS GRAPHIC ORGANIZER

Directions: In the space provided, list all of the strengths and "gifts/talents" you think you demonstrate. This is not the time to by shy—list them all, no matter how silly you feel.

STRENGTHS	GIFTS/TALENTS
Honesty	Calculating math problems

STRENGTHS WORD BANK

Artistic	Daring	Leader
Athletic	Dedicated	Mature
Adventurous	Energetic	Motivated
Bright	Focused	Risk taker
Brave	Forgiving	Self-reliant
Charismatic	Honest	Sincere
Clever	Independent	Thoughtful
Compassionate	Innovative	Trustworthy
Curious	Inquisitive	Unique

LESSON 15
I THINK I CAN

OBJECTIVE

By the end of the lesson, students will be able to:

- understand what self-talk is and the impact of self-limiting beliefs,
- identify personal self-limiting beliefs and replace them with balanced talk, and
- use a strategy for identifying and replacing negative self-talk.

GUIDING QUESTIONS FOR STUDENTS

- What messages do I give myself? Are these messages accurate?
- Can I improve my productivity and emotional balance when I replace negative self-talk with balanced talk?

GUIDING PRINCIPLES

Developing a foundation of successful daily habits involves recognizing the role self-talk has on behavior and emotional balance. Negative self-talk causes self-limiting beliefs that can significantly inhibit the gifted individual's ability to maximize his or her potential. Learning to both recognize and change this defeatist thinking is the key to developing a habit of optimism and resilience.

MATERIALS

- Handout 15.1: Proof Graphic Organizer
- Handout 15.2: Thinking Brain
- Crayons, colored pencils, or other writing utensils for students
- Whiteboard, flipchart, or smart board for discussion

INTRODUCTION

Introduce guiding principles and vocabulary. Give each student the handouts.

ACTIVITY

- Introduce the concept of self-talk and the influence self-talk has on human behavior. Cite examples of how negative self-talk can lead to defeatist behaviors and how optimism can lead to successful behaviors.

■ Instruct students to complete the Proof Graphic Organizer. Provide one example for the students and ask them to complete the rest of the graphic organizer with 2–3 examples of negative self-talk in which they have engaged.

■ Ask students to brainstorm balanced talk ideas to replace their negative beliefs.

■ Using the Thinking Brain handout, instruct students to create an infographic highlighting both self-defeatist thinking and positive thinking. Decorate the graphic as time permits.

DISCUSSION

Discuss the importance of positive thinking. Use the following discussion questions to aid the conversation:

■ How does negative self-talk impact behavior and performance?

■ Did the "Proof" strategy help you change your thinking?

■ How can you become more aware of defeatist thinking in the future?

ASSESSMENT

Evaluate the students' projects based on appropriate standards.

PROOF GRAPHIC ORGANIZER

Directions: Complete as indicated in the lesson:

Negative thoughts: _____

What proof do you have that the thought is correct?

_____

_____

Can you find something that contradicts this thought?

_____

_____

What would you advise your best friend if he or she had this thought?

_____

_____

Does this thought help you?

_____

_____

How will you feel about this in 3 months? In 6 months?

_____

_____

Create a balanced thought to replace the negative thought:

_____

_____

THINKING BRAIN

Directions: Either use the template below or something of your own design to create a graphic representation of what you've learned about creating balanced self-messages.

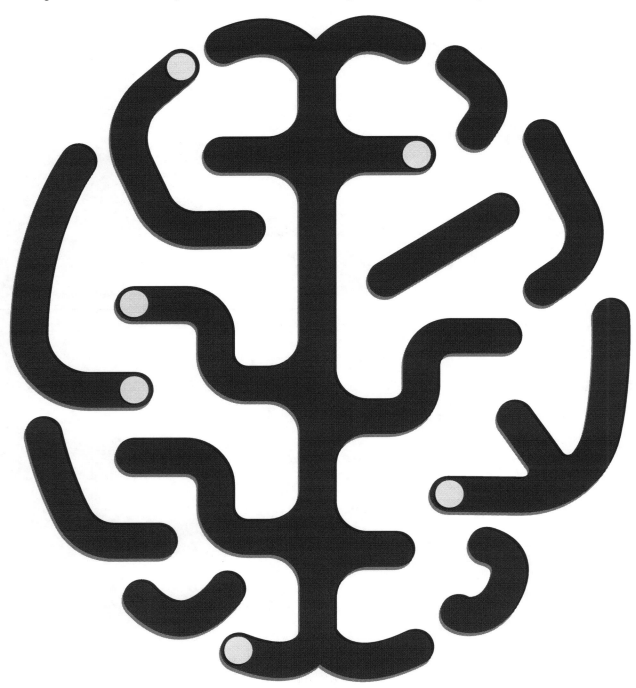

LESSON 16
I'M PROUD OF . . .

OBJECTIVE

By the end of the lesson, students will be able to:

- identify individual accomplishments, and
- explain why it is important to recognize and celebrate individual accomplishments.

GUIDING QUESTIONS FOR STUDENTS

- What are my accomplishments? How do I celebrate them?

GUIDING PRINCIPLES

Gifted individuals often have high expectations for themselves. As a result, gifted individuals seldom recognize their accomplishments or celebrate them. They consider the accomplishment a given and often focus on the ways in which they can improve their performance. Although task analysis is a positive trait, when taken to this extreme it does not serve the gifted individual. Taking a moment to recognize and celebrate individual accomplishments is important and sets the stage for increased performance. This adjustment and focus from neutral or negative to positive also improves gifted individuals' coping strategies and helps to balance their expectations.

MATERIALS

- Writing journal or notebook
- Crayons, colored pencils, or other writing utensils for students
- Whiteboard, flipchart, or smart board for discussion

INTRODUCTION

Arrange desks in groups 2–4. Introduce guiding principles and any required vocabulary. Give each student a writing journal or notebook.

ACTIVITY

- Discuss accomplishments and expectations. Provide an example or use a story to assist with understanding.

■ Ask students to think of 1–2 accomplishments from the past week. Ask students to write down their accomplishments in their journal. Invite students to share some of their accomplishments with the group.

■ Instruct students to brainstorm ways to celebrate accomplishments.

■ Decide on a timeframe for journaling. One to 2 months is typically a good amount of time. Ask students to write 1–3 accomplishments nightly in their journal. Invite students to bring their journal in weekly and share their accomplishments. (*Note.* You may want to set up a weekly sharing time for students to celebrate accomplishments. This lesson can tie to goal-setting lessons found later in the book.)

DISCUSSION

Discuss the importance of focusing on accomplishments. Include a discussion of any barriers to this focus. Use the following discussion questions to aid the conversation:

■ Was it easy or difficult to focus on accomplishments? Why?

■ Why is it important to think of accomplishments even when they are small?

■ Why is celebration important? What are the benefits to celebrating accomplishments?

ASSESSMENT

Evaluate the students' responses based on appropriate standards.

LESSON 17
FAILURE ISN'T THE END

OBJECTIVE

By the end of the lesson, students will be able to:

- explain the benefits of failure,
- identify examples of success that followed failure, and
- explain the concepts of failure, success, resiliency, and motivation.

GUIDING QUESTIONS FOR STUDENTS

- How does failure often lead to success?
- What are some examples of this concept?

GUIDING PRINCIPLES

Few accomplished people have ever achieved success without first experiencing failure. These people understood that failure was not the end of a journey. It was very often the beginning. Gifted individuals sometimes struggle with failure. Issues of perfectionism and poor risk-taking can inhibit their ability to persevere. Finding motivation after failure is key to developing the resiliency needed in life.

MATERIALS

- Handout 17.1: Failure Is the Beginning
- Computer with Internet access
- Large poster board or digital vision board
- Crayons, colored pencils, or other writing utensils for students
- Whiteboard, flipchart, or smart board for discussion

INTRODUCTION

Arrange desks into groups of 2–4. Introduce guiding principles. Give each student the handout and computer access (with Internet).

ACTIVITY

- Discuss the concepts of failure, success, resiliency, and motivation. Ask students to brainstorm examples of each concept.

▪▪ Using the worksheet, invite students to research individuals who have reached success only after failure.

▪▪ Instruct students to find 1–3 motivational quotes from their chosen people.

▪▪ Instruct students to make a poster illustrating their famous person, how they overcame failure, and a minimum of one motivational quote. These posters can be hung around the room or developed into a class blog post.

DISCUSSION

Discuss how the individuals studied overcame adversity. Focus on how their examples can be incorporated into the students' daily lives. Use the following discussion questions to aid the conversation:

▪▪ How did failure lead to success?

▪▪ Are there examples of failure leading to success in your own life?

▪▪ What can be learned by studying the lives of people who have overcome adversity?

ASSESSMENT

Evaluate the students' projects based on appropriate standards.

Name: _____ Date: _____

FAILURE IS THE BEGINNING

Directions: Complete the questions as you conduct your research.

Name of person being researched: _____

What did he or she "fail" at?

_____

_____

_____

How did the "failure" lead to future successes?

_____

_____

_____

What do you think the person learned from failure?

_____

_____

_____

How would you have felt about failing?

_____

_____

_____

List a motivational quote or two from this person.

_____

_____

_____

LESSON 18
RESPONSIBLE OR NOT

OBJECTIVE

By the end of the lesson, students will be able to:
- define four types of responsibility: personal, social, legal, moral;
- understand the components of responsibility: accountability, courage, and self-control; and
- evaluate their current level of responsibility in their lives.

GUIDING QUESTIONS FOR STUDENTS
- What does responsibility mean to me?
- How do I demonstrate that I am a responsible person?

GUIDING PRINCIPLES

Personal responsibility is a key component of developing emotional intelligence. Sometimes it's difficult to accept responsibility for our actions, especially if we think we've done something that breaks the rules or is against the norm. Gifted individuals also struggle with personal responsibility at times, often using their strong communication skills to redirect blame and abdicate responsibility. Understanding the different types of responsibility, as well as the factors that influence a person's ability to be responsible, is an important step in developing character and appropriate sense of responsibility.

MATERIALS
- Handout 18.1: Responsibility
- Seven large pieces of blank paper hung around the room, labeled with the types and components of responsibility
- Journal or notebook
- Crayons, colored pencils, or other writing utensils for students
- Whiteboard, flipchart, or smart board for discussion

INTRODUCTION

Arrange desks in groups of 2–4. Introduce guiding principles and any necessary vocabulary. Pass out Handout 18.1.

ACTIVITY

- Introduce the four types of responsibility. Ask table groups to brainstorm different activities to fit within each group and write them on their worksheet. Ask students to walk around the room and put their ideas on the appropriate sheets of paper.

- Introduce the three components of responsibility. Ask table groups to brainstorm different actions that demonstrate the components. Ask students to walk around the room and put their ideas on the appropriate sheets of paper.

- Assign each group one type of responsibility. Using the information discussed in class, instruct groups to develop a brief poster highlighting the definition and components of their assigned type of responsibility. Groups may decorate the posters as desired.

- Provide each student with a journal or notebook and ask them to write down any activities in which they demonstrated responsibility and any in which they failed to demonstrate responsibility. Ask students to return the journals in one week. When the journals are returned, discuss the activity with the students. Ask them if there were any surprises and to share their personal experiences. (*Note.* This extension activity is not required, but will personalize the lesson for the students.)

DISCUSSION

Discuss the importance of demonstrating responsibility and some difficulties gifted children may have with this. Use the following discussion questions to aid the conversation:

- Are there some types of responsibility that are more difficult than others to demonstrate?
- Which of the components of responsibility is the most difficult to develop?
- What are some ways you can improve your ability to be responsible?

ASSESSMENT

Evaluate the students' projects based on appropriate standards.

RESPONSIBILITY

Directions: Complete as indicated in the activity.

TYPES OF RESPONSIBILITY

Personal:	Legal:
Social:	Moral:

COMPONENTS OF RESPONSIBILITY

Accountability:
Courage:
Self-control:

LESSON 19
THE ART OF MAKING DECISIONS

OBJECTIVE

By the end of the lesson, students will be able to:

- understand the components of making decisions,
- practice making decisions, and
- explain how goals, personal preferences, and values can impact decision making.

GUIDING QUESTIONS FOR STUDENTS

- What are the components involved with decision making?
- How can I learn to make good decisions?

GUIDING PRINCIPLES

- Making decisions can be challenging, especially if you are good at seeing many alternatives for each decision. Knowing what's important to you, what you hope to achieve, and how to achieve it can help you discern between potential outcomes. This is especially important when making big decisions.
- The decision-making strategy for this lesson involves the following steps:
  - Clearly define the decision to be made.
  - Identify your desired outcome.
  - Review the information you have related to the decision. Gather additional information if needed.
  - Examine alternative outcomes for the decision and evaluate the impact of the decision on yourself and others.
  - If the decision is long-term or requires several steps to accomplish, develop an action plan.

MATERIALS

- Handout 19.1: Decisions
- Handout 19.2: Decision Tree Graphic Organizer
- Crayons, colored pencils, or other writing utensils for students
- Whiteboard, flipchart, or smart board for discussion

INTRODUCTION

Introduce guiding principles and any necessary vocabulary. Give each student the handouts.

ACTIVITY

- Introduce students to the decision-making process. Ask for examples from the students of how each step can be accomplished. Instruct students to complete Handout 19.1 throughout the discussion.
- Using the Decision Tree, ask students to pick one decision and complete the tree by writing down each step and its potential outcomes.
- Ask students to share their decision trees with a partner.

DISCUSSION

Discuss the importance of decision making. Use the following questions to guide the conversation:

- What did you learn from making your decision trees?
- What are the most difficult aspects of decision making?
- Why is it important to know the alternatives for each decision?

ASSESSMENT

Instruct students to complete the questions on the decision tree. Evaluate the students' projects based on appropriate standards.

DECISIONS

Directions: Complete as you discuss the decision-making process.

STEP	ACTION
1. Define the decision clearly.	
2. Identify what you want to happen.	
3. Gather information you need to make the decision.	
4. Examine all possible outcomes based on the different decisions you could make.	
5. Choose one decision.	

DECISION TREE GRAPHIC ORGANIZER

Directions: Complete the graphic organizer for the initial decision.

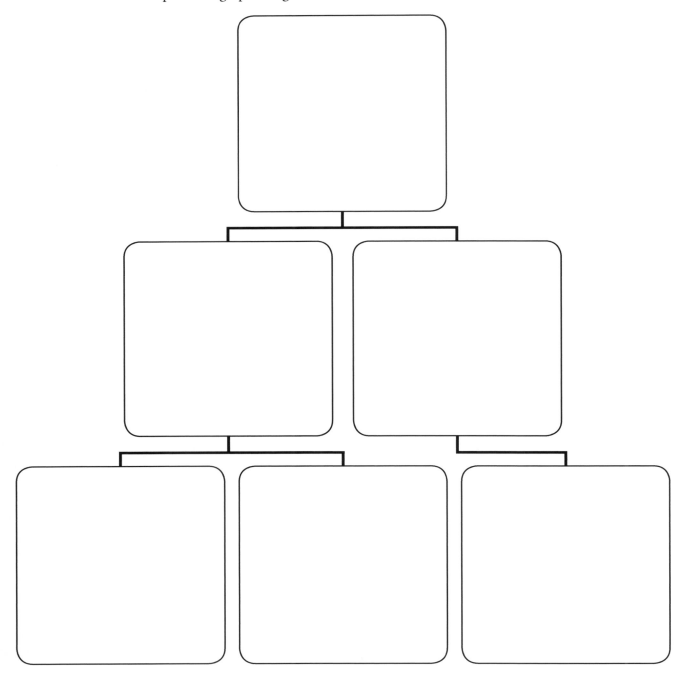

LESSON 20
LET'S RELAX

OBJECTIVE

By the end of the lesson, students will be able to:

- identify specific strategies for relaxation, and
- explain how to utilize relaxation strategies.

GUIDING QUESTIONS FOR STUDENTS

- What relaxation strategies work best for me?

GUIDING PRINCIPLES

Gifted individuals often experience high levels of emotional intensity. This can be particularly true with regard to stress and anxiety. Learning how to relax is an important skill to incorporate into your daily habits. Furthermore, knowing a variety of ways to de-stress is key to improving your ability to cope with life's frustrating or stressful moments.

MATERIALS

- Handout 20.1: Relax Now!
- 3 x 5 index cards
- Hole punch
- String
- Crayons, colored pencils, or other writing utensils for students
- Whiteboard, flipchart, or smart board for discussion

INTRODUCTION

Arrange desks in groups of 2–4. Provide each table group with art supplies, string, a hole punch, and enough cards for each student to have 3–5 cards. Give each student the worksheet.

ACTIVITY

- Discuss the concept of relaxation. Invite students to provide examples of ways they relax.

■ Using the worksheet, instruct the students to pick 3–5 relaxation strategies they commit to using. Instruct students to draw a graphic representation of the technique on one side of the cards, one strategy per card. On the reverse side, ask students to write the steps for the technique. Specific instructions for each technique can be found on the worksheet.

■ When the students have created their cards, instruct them to punch a hole in each card and string them together to make a ring.

■ Ask students to complete the questions on the handout. Although the students are sitting in groups, the handout must reflect each student's individual thoughts.

DISCUSSION

Discuss the importance of learning to relax. Use the following discussion questions to aid the conversation:

■ Why is relaxation difficult for some people to achieve?

■ Why is it important to learn many ways to achieve a relaxed state of mind?

■ What strategies work best for you? What strategies are the least helpful?

ASSESSMENT

Evaluate the students' projects based on appropriate standards.

Name: _____ Date: _____

RELAX NOW!

Directions: Use the worksheet to discover new ways to relax, as indicated in the activity.

Deep Breathing	Breathing Colors	Yoga/Stretching
1. Take a deep breath. 2. Hold it for a few moments. 3. Exhale through your mouth. 4. Repeat slowly until you feel more relaxed.	1. Pick a calming color. 2. Take a slow, deep breath and imagine you are breathing in the color. 3. Exhale through your mouth imagining an ugly color. 4. Repeat deep breathing until you can "see" your calming color when you exhale.	Take a few moments to practice deep stretching and/or yoga.
Tense and Release	**Exercise**	**Mindfulness**
1. Tighten your face and scrunch up your nose. Hold for a few moments and then release. Repeat three times. 2. Tighten your jaw by pretending you are biting down on something. Hold for a few moments and then release. Repeat three times. 3. Repeat this process with your shoulders, your arms and hands, and finally your legs and feet.	Take a walk or engage in some form of physical exercise for 20–30 minutes.	1. Take a few moments to clear your thoughts. 2. Focus on your breathing. 3. Take five deep breaths, focusing only on your breath.
Laugh	**Toe Tense**	**Talk With a Friend**
Laughter and humor are instant stress busters. As is smiling!	1. Lay down and stretch your toes back toward your face. 2. Relax your feet for a moment. 3. Repeat three to five times.	Connecting with others can release your stress. So reach out and connect with a close friend.

LESSON 21
OVERLOADED

OBJECTIVE

By the end of the lesson, students will be able to:

- recognize the physical, mental, and emotional indicators of being overwhelmed;
- analyze previous coping strategy usage; and
- refine their personal list of coping strategies.

GUIDING QUESTIONS FOR STUDENTS

- What physical, mental, and emotional signs tell me when I am overwhelmed?
- What coping strategies help me regain balance?

GUIDING PRINCIPLES

- Everyone feels overwhelmed from time to time. With gifted individuals, a period of overload can easily result in extreme, sometimes paralyzing, emotional reactions.
- Knowing when you are becoming overwhelmed and what to do to regain control is important to achieving emotional balance.
- Mindfulness is an important step in being able to recognize the physical, mental, and emotional indicators of being overwhelmed.

MATERIALS

- Handout 21.1: My Stress Indicators Graphic Organizer
- Notebook and/or journal for each student
- Crayons, colored pencils, or other writing utensils for students
- Whiteboard, flipchart, or smart board for discussion

INTRODUCTION

Create groups of 2–4 students. Give each student a graphic organizer. Introduce guiding principles and any needed vocabulary.

ACTIVITY

- Discuss what it means to be overwhelmed in terms of physical, mental, and emotional signs. Use a movie clip or book reference to provide an example as needed.
- Working in small groups, ask each student to share a time when he or she felt overwhelmed. Ask students to complete the graphic organizer, describing the physical, mental, and emotional signs.
- Ask each group to develop a skit that shows the different signs of stress. One by one, ask groups to act out their scenes while the other groups watch. After each scene is demonstrated, ask the other students to identify the physical, mental, and emotional signs that suggest the characters were overwhelmed.

DISCUSSION

Discuss why it is important to learn the signs that a person is feeling overwhelmed. Discuss how to regain emotional control after being overwhelmed. Use the following discussion questions to aid the conversation:

- Why do people become overwhelmed?
- How can you tell you're headed for overload?
- What can you do to bring your emotions back under control once you've reached overload?

ASSESSMENT

Evaluate the students' responses and skits based on appropriate standards.

HANDOUT 21.1

MY STRESS INDICATORS
GRAPHIC ORGANIZER

Directions: Complete as directed.

EVENT	PHYSICAL SIGNS	MENTAL SIGNS	EMOTIONAL SIGNS

LESSON 22
THIS IS STRESSING ME OUT!

OBJECTIVE

By the end of the lesson, students will be able to:
- identify triggers for stress, and
- identify personal stress triggers and possible coping strategies.

GUIDING QUESTIONS FOR STUDENTS

- What events make me stressed?
- What can I do to manage my stress?

GUIDING PRINCIPLES

Everyone feel stress from time to time. However, not everyone feels the same amount of stress in various situations. Before you can learn to cope with stress, you must learn what events or situations cause stress and the degree of stressed caused by each. Then you can focus on coping strategies to reduce or eliminate the stress.

MATERIALS

- Handout 22.1: My Stress
- Five large pieces of paper
- Crayons, colored pencils, or other writing utensils for students
- Whiteboard, flipchart, or smart board for discussion

INTRODUCTION

Write the following titles on the pieces of paper: Stress at School, Stress at Home, Stress From Friends, Stress From the Future, Stress From the BIG Things. Mount them around the room. Introduce guiding principles and vocabulary. Give each student Handout 22.1.

ACTIVITY

- Discuss what stress is and the physical, mental, and emotional indicators of stress. Discuss what kinds of things can lead to stress. Point out the five most common areas of stress indicated on the papers around the room. Have students provide one or two examples of each.

- Ask students to walk around the room and add examples to each of the pieces of paper. Leave the papers hanging throughout the lesson.
- When students have filled each paper, ask them to return to their seats and complete the worksheet with examples of things that cause them stress. They can use the examples around the room or come up with their own.
- Ask students to rate the amount of stress each event causes from 1–5, with 1 being the least amount of stress and 5 being the most.

DISCUSSION

Discuss the different lists the students made. Discuss the idea of controlling and/or changing the event to reduce the amount of stress the event causes. Ask students to reflect on their event list and rate the amount of control the student has to alter/change the event from 1–5, with 1 being no control to 5 being the most control.

ASSESSMENT

Evaluate the students' responses based on appropriate standards.

Name:_____ Date: _____

MY STRESS

Directions: Complete the table with the things that cause you stress.

STRESS EVENT/TRIGGER	STRESS RATING: 1–5 (1 = THE LEAST STRESS; 5 = THE MOST STRESS)	PERSONAL CONTROL RATING: 1–5 (1 = NO CONTROL; 5 = MAX CONTROL)

LESSON 23
A STROLL THROUGH MY STRESS

OBJECTIVE

By the end of the lesson, students will be able to:

- understand the physical, mental, and emotional indicators of stress;
- explain how stress personally impacts them physically, mentally, and emotionally; and
- identify 1–3 strategies to reduce or relieve stress.

GUIDING QUESTION FOR STUDENTS

- How does stress impact my body, my mind, and my emotions?

GUIDING PRINCIPLES

Emotional intensity is a common aspect of giftedness. This intensity can heighten the signs of stress and frustration experienced by gifted individuals. Understanding the specific ways stress impacts your body, your mind, and your emotions is an important first step to managing your emotions and balancing emotional intensity.

MATERIALS

- Handout 23.1: Mind-Body
- Three large pieces of paper hung around the room, one for each: physical symptoms, mental symptoms, emotional symptoms
- Crayons, colored pencils, or other writing utensils for students
- Whiteboard, flipchart, or smart board for discussion

INTRODUCTION

Introduce guiding principles and any required vocabulary. Give each student the handout.

ACTIVITY

- Discuss a definition for stress and the physical, mental, and emotional symptoms of stress. Invite students to write down various symptoms of stress under the specific headings around the room.

- Ask students to remember a time when they felt high levels of stress. Instruct them to complete Section 1 of the handout based on this memory.
- Discuss how students demonstrated stress in their bodies, in their minds, and in their behavior.
- Based on the discussion, ask students to brainstorm ways to reduce the symptoms of stress. (Note: As an extension activity, invite students to keep a journal of stress symptoms they experience throughout the week. Remind students that stress can be felt when doing pleasurable activities, as well as more negative activities.)

DISCUSSION

Discuss the students' personal experiences with stress. Use the following discussion questions to aid the conversation:

- How do you demonstrate stress?
- Now that you know what your personal stress response is, do you think you will be able to manage the symptoms better? Why or why not?
- What do you think is most important in managing your stress symptoms? Why?

ASSESSMENT

Evaluate the students' responses based on appropriate standards.

MIND-BODY

Directions: Complete this worksheet with a specific event and *your* specific stress signs.

EVENT	PHYSICAL SIGNS	MENTAL SIGNS	EMOTIONAL SIGNS

Using a relaxation strategy, can you change your physical, mental, and emotional indicators of stress?

_____

_____

_____

_____

_____

_____

_____

_____

_____

_____

LESSON 24
ALL ABOUT BALANCE

OBJECTIVE

By the end of the lesson, students will be able to:
- understand what it means to live "in balance,"
- identify what areas of balance need improvement, and
- create goals related to balanced living.

GUIDING QUESTIONS FOR STUDENTS

- What are the key components to balanced living?
- How do my current lifestyle choices relate to balanced living?
- What are my areas of strength and improvement?

GUIDING PRINCIPLES

We live hectic lives. As a result, most people—including gifted individuals—fail to live balanced lives in terms of eating habits, rest, exercise, and recreational activities. For gifted individuals, this can be particularly problematic, as an out-of-sync life can exacerbate areas of overexcitability. It is important for gifted individuals to take stock from time to time and recognize which aspects of their lifestyle are balanced and which require adjustments.

MATERIALS

- Handout 24.1: Success Secret #15 From *101 Success Secrets for Gifted Children*
- Handout 24.2: Am I Balanced? Graphic Organizer
- Handout 24.3: Pie Chart
- Crayons, colored pencils, or other writing utensils for students
- Whiteboard, flipchart, or smart board for discussion

INTRODUCTION

Arrange desks into groups of 2–4. Provide students with copies of the handouts. Introduce guiding principles and any needed vocabulary.

ACTIVITY

■ Instruct students to read Success Secret #15 (Handout 24.1) and discuss as a group. Are there any areas of disagreement in the group? Are there some things that need to be added?

■ Ask students to complete the graphic organizer in Handout 24.2. Students can work in groups, but the organizer needs to reflect their personal reflections on their own lives.

■ Share the organizers as a large group. Discuss areas of difficulty that may have surfaced, as well as areas of balance.

■ Ask students to complete the pie chart in Handout 24.3, graphing how much time is spent in the various areas of life.

■ Ask students to identify 1–2 areas of improvement and write a goal for themselves in that area.

DISCUSSION

As a group, discuss why balanced living is so important. Also discuss the types of barriers a student might encounter when trying to be more balanced in his or her lifestyle. Use the following discussion questions to aid the conversation:

■ How do you spend your time currently? Are there areas you'd like to improve?

■ What are some of the reasons it can be difficult to remain in balance?

■ How can you work around barriers or other difficulties?

■ If you could improve in one area, what would it be?

ASSESSMENT

Instruct students to write a goal and an action plan for achieving the goal. Evaluate the students' projects based on appropriate standards.

SUCCESS SECRET #15 FROM 101 SUCCESS SECRETS FOR GIFTED KIDS

SUCCESS SECRET #15 Remember to take care of yourself.

Being a gifted kid is both great and difficult. But, regardless of whether you're having an easy time with your giftedness or a hard time, there are a few things you can do to manage your life better. The biggest thing is taking good care of yourself. No one copes well when he is tired, hungry, or stressed. Remembering to make *you* a priority in your life is essential to being successful now and later on.

TIPS FOR TAKING CARE OF YOURSELF

1. **Get plenty of rest**. Most kids your age require at least 8 hours every night. Developing a bedtime routine can help if you have a hard time getting to sleep at night.
2. **Eat healthy foods**. Junk food may taste good, but it can really work against your brain functioning and overall health. Learn about good food choices and commit to eating healthy every day.
3. **Stay active**. Exercise is an essential part of taking care of yourself. Most schools don't have daily P.E., so it is really important to spend a part of every day being active. Dance, jumping rope, playing ball—all of these forms of exercise will improve your brain functioning, keep you healthy, and make it easier to get to sleep at night. Not only that, but exercise is one of the best ways to combat stress.
4. **Relax**. We live in a very busy world. Learning to relax a little every day can help rejuvenate our minds and our bodies. Try deep breathing, yoga, prayer, or just sitting in silence for a few minutes every day.
5. **Play**. Life isn't just about work, especially when you're a kid. It is easy to get too busy with school and your extra activities to remember to play. But, playing is just as important as everything else. So find a way to carve out a few minutes of playtime. You can play with a friend, a pet, or your parents. Just a few minutes a day is all you need to stay in balance.

Note. From *101 Success Secrets for Gifted Kids* (pp. 24–25), by Christine Fonseca, 2011, Waco, TX: Prufrock Press. Copyright 2011 Prufrock Press Inc. Reprinted with permission.

Name:_____ Date: _____

AM I BALANCED?
GRAPHIC ORGANIZER

Directions: Complete as directed.

HEALTHY HABIT	HOW I SHOW IT	HOW OFTEN I DO THIS EVERY WEEK
Healthy eating		
Sleep/Rest		
Relaxation		
Play/Recreation		
School/Work		
Other commitments:		

PIE CHART

Directions: The circle below represents 24 hours. Divide the pie based on how much time to spend doing each of the healthy habits as indicated on Handout 24.2.

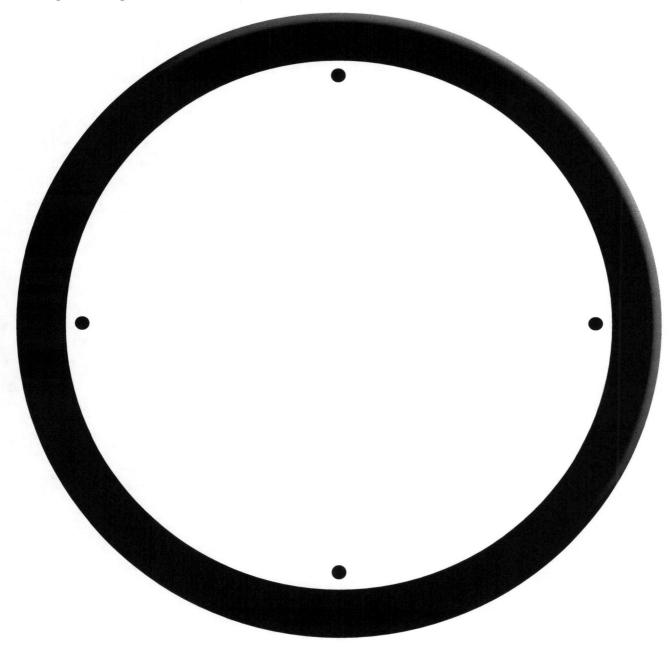

CHAPTER 8

Unit IV
The Art of
Bouncing Back

Developing resiliency skills is an important aspect of social-emotional development and learning (CASEL, n.d.; Hébert, 2011; Kitano & Lewis, 2005; Neihart, 2002; Prince-Embury, 2005). The components of resiliency—mastery, connections, and emotional balance—can be difficult for some children to develop (Fonseca, 2014). This is particularly true for gifted children (Neihart, 2002). Issues involving perfectionism, rigid thinking, and underdeveloped relationship skills can weaken the development of resiliency in gifted children and inhibit risk-taking—all of which can result in underperformance (Durlak et al., 2010; Siegle, 2013).

Utilizing discussion groups and journaling, as well as improving communication skills, this unit focuses on enhancing the development of a positive mindset by supporting the components of resiliency and promoting academic risk-taking in preparation for the next unit focused on talent development.

UNIT OVERVIEW

The 11 lessons in this unit cover four broad skill areas as follows:

- *Adaptability skills* (Lessons 25–27): Considered one of the cornerstones to resiliency (Prince-Embury, 2005), the three lessons in this section focus on perspective taking, creativity, and self-reflection.
- *Developing relationships* (Lessons 28–30): These lessons focus on cultivating relationships and friendships, conflict resolution, and developing support systems.

▓ *Communication skills* (Lessons 31–33): The heart of this unit is communication. The lessons delve into developing effective speaking and listening skills, as well as the impact of communication roadblocks.

▓ *Leadership and collaboration* (Lessons 34–35): These last few lessons introduce leadership skills and collaboration.

As with the previous units, the overall value of the lessons is enhanced through diversity. Adding media sources for examples will also deepen the content of each lesson. Use the questions to allow for a deeper, personal exploration of discussion topics.

EXTENSION OPPORTUNITIES

Some potential extension activities that can build on the lessons in this unit include the following:

▓ Write a story from a new perspective.

▓ Complete Random Acts Of Kindness service projects.

▓ Develop curricula for younger students and teach it through mentoring.

▓ Work on a semester-long collaborative project centered around students' talents and/or interests.

LESSON 25
NEW PERSPECTIVES

OBJECTIVE

By the end of the lesson, students will be able to:

- understand the importance of perspective taking with reference to emotional intelligence and resiliency, and
- be able to demonstrate perspective taking.

GUIDING QUESTIONS FOR STUDENTS

- Why is it important to understand another person's point of view?
- What can be gained by seeing things from a fresh perspective?

GUIDING PRINCIPLES

Seeing the world from multiple perspectives is an important key to the development of empathy. By understanding the point of view of others, you can begin to understand why people do the things they do. Additionally, perspective taking enables you to develop problem-solving and relationship skills. Gifted individuals can develop empathy for others by practicing perspective-taking skills.

MATERIALS

- Paper for a poster
- Crayons, colored pencils, or other writing utensils for students
- Whiteboard, flipchart, or smart board for discussion

INTRODUCTION

Arrange the desks into groups of 2–4. Introduce the guiding principles.

ACTIVITY

- Ask each group to retell a common fairy tale from a different point of view.
- Give each group 10 minutes to develop a skit based on retelling the fairy tale from the new character's perspective. Encourage creativity.
- Ask each group to perform the skit for the class. (*Note.* As an alternative to the skit, students can rewrite the story from the perspective of the new character

in story book format. This is a good option for introverted children or those with social anxiety disorder.)

DISCUSSION

Discuss the importance of taking fresh perspective to the development of empathy. Discuss other stories or movies that take new perspectives on old stories. What can be learned from these works? Use the following discussion questions to aid the conversation:

- What did you learn from your experience taking a new perspective?
- How can this help you in the future in terms of relationships?
- How do the concepts of empathy or conflict resolution relate to perspective taking?

ASSESSMENT

Develop a poster with five tips for taking a fresh perspective. The poster can be created at that time or in subsequent sessions. Evaluate the students' responses based on appropriate standards.

LESSON 26
101 ROADS

OBJECTIVE

By the end of the lesson, students will be able to:

- ▥ identify 2–4 ways to achieve a variety of goals, and
- ▥ explain why it is important to demonstrate flexible thinking and adaptation skills.

GUIDING QUESTIONS FOR STUDENTS

- ▥ Why is it important to find many ways to achieve a goal?
- ▥ What does it mean to be adaptable or flexible?

GUIDING PRINCIPLES

A key component to developing resiliency is adaptability or flexible thinking. Understanding that things seldom go exactly as planned is the first step in developing adaptation skills. Being able to identify multiple ways to accomplish a task or achieve goals is another way to develop flexible thinking skills.

MATERIALS

- ▥ Handout 26.1: 101 Roads
- ▥ Common classroom items, including pencils, staples, paperclips, etc.
- ▥ Crayons, colored pencils, or other writing utensils for students
- ▥ Whiteboard, flipchart, or smart board for discussion

INTRODUCTION

Arrange desks in groups of 2–4. Place 1–2 classroom objects on each group's table. Introduce guiding principles and any required vocabulary. Provide each student with the handout.

ACTIVITY

- ▥ Discuss the idea that there are many ways to complete a task.
- ▥ Instruct each group to develop 2–3 ways to explain how to use the group's common classroom item. They should think of new ways to use the item,

beyond the ways it is typically used within the classroom. Invite groups to share 1–2 examples with the class.

- Ask the class to brainstorm why it's important to be able to achieve tasks in a variety of ways. Tie this idea into developing goals.
- Provide each group with a small task or goal for the classroom (a way to take attendance more efficiently, etc.). Ask the group to brainstorm 2–3 different ways to complete the task or achieve the goal.
- Using the worksheet, instruct students to develop 2–3 goals and 2–3 ways to achieve each goal. Although students may work in groups, the worksheet must reflect each student's individual thoughts.

DISCUSSION

Discuss the importance of flexible thinking and adaptation. Use the following discussion questions to aid the conversation:

- How does flexible thinking and adaptation help you?
- How did the demonstration with the classroom objects change or enhance your ideas about flexible thinking?
- How will you use flexible thinking in the future?

ASSESSMENT

Evaluate the students' worksheets based on appropriate standards.

Name:_____ Date: _____

101 ROADS

Directions: Brainstorm goals, then several ways you can achieve them.

GOALS	ACTION PLAN #1	ACTION PLAN #2

LESSON 27
THE ART OF GRATITUDE

OBJECTIVE

By the end of the lesson, students will be able to:

- understand why gratitude is an important aspect of resiliency,
- explain the importance of gratitude to others, and
- demonstrate the use of a gratitude journal.

GUIDING QUESTIONS FOR STUDENTS

- Why is gratitude important?
- How can I demonstrate gratitude in my daily life?

GUIDING PRINCIPLES

Focusing on gratitude is more than a nice idea. Gratitude improves negative self-talk by shifting the focus from defeatist victimization to positive abundance. It creates an optimistic mindset that is linked to improved resiliency. Cultivating the habit of being grateful can be a challenge at times. It is important to set a little time aside daily to reflect on the positive things in our lives. Learning to adjust our focus in this way can significantly improve our mood.

MATERIALS

- Writing journal or notebook
- Crayons, colored pencils, or other writing utensils for students
- Whiteboard, flipchart, or smart board for discussion

INTRODUCTION

Introduce guiding principles and any needed vocabulary. Give each student a journal.

ACTIVITY

- Discuss the difference between half-empty, defeatist thinking and half-full, optimistic or grateful thinking. Provide examples of how to switch from lack to abundance.

- Write three negative statements on the board and ask students to shift them to positive statements. Discuss the connection between practicing gratitude and optimistic thinking.
- Using the journal, ask students to write 1–3 things they are grateful for. Invite students to share their answers. (*Note.* To extend the activity, ask students to maintain the journal for at least 3 weeks. Invite students to share some of their entries and reflect on the activity in small groups.)

DISCUSSION

As a group, discuss the impact of shifting thoughts from negative to positive. Use the following discussion questions to aid the conversation:

- What did you notice about how you felt when you shifted from negative to positive thinking?
- How does focusing on gratitude improve your general attitude?
- What is the important lesson to be learned from grateful thinking and being optimistic?

ASSESSMENT

Working in small groups, instruct students to create a class blog post or an infographic explaining the importance of being grateful. Evaluate the students' projects based on appropriate standards.

LESSON 28
ME AND MY FRIENDS

OBJECTIVE

By the end of the lesson, students will be able to:

- identify the qualities of a good friend,
- identify the qualities of friendship their friends demonstrate, and
- develop a strategy for dealing with friendship conflict.

GUIDING QUESTIONS FOR STUDENTS

- What qualities of friendship are most important to me?
- How do my friends demonstrate these qualities?

GUIDING PRINCIPLES

One of the basic factors of resiliency is the development of strong, healthy relationships. Friendship can meet this need and help individuals to develop both resiliency and social skills. These skills can be difficult for gifted individuals to learn. Often misunderstood by peers, learning how to develop and maintain friendships across a large cross-section of peers is one way for gifted individuals to build resiliency. Learning how to manage friendship conflicts by refocusing on the positive attributes of the relationship is another.

MATERIALS

- Handout 28.1: Friendship Graphic Organizer
- 3 x 5 cards and string
- Magazines for clipping, or access to graphic images
- Crayons, colored pencils, or other writing utensils for students
- Whiteboard, flipchart, or smart board for discussion

INTRODUCTION

Provide students with graphic organizer, cards, string, and art supplies. Introduce guiding principles and any needed vocabulary.

ACTIVITY

- Discuss the qualities of a healthy friendship. Ask students to brainstorm different traits. Write the list on large paper or the smart board.
- Ask students to complete Section 1 of the graphic organizer, focusing on one or two friends.
- Instruct students to make a card for each friend, focusing on positive traits and friendship qualities. Decorate the cards as desired.
- Ask students to brainstorm ways to remember these positive attributes when they are in conflict with their friends. Make a list of the strategies discussed.
- Instruct students to pick one or two strategies and write them on the back of the cards.

DISCUSSION

Discuss the importance of friendships. Discuss the different roles friendships have in our lives, as well as the types of conflicts that can happen. Use the following discussion questions to aid the conversation:

- Is it hard to make friends at times? Why or why not?
- How do you know you are a *good* friend? What does being a *good* friend mean?
- What strategies have worked best for you when you and your friends experience conflict?

ASSESSMENT

Instruct students to pick one of the friends from the friendship cards and write a letter to the friend to thank him or her for his or her friendship. Include details about the friendship, qualities that make the friendship important, and ways to maintain the friendship. The letters do *not* need to be delivered to the friend—this is just an exercise. Evaluate the students' projects based on appropriate standards.

FRIENDSHIP GRAPHIC ORGANIZER

Directions: Complete based on the activity.

NAME OF FRIEND	HOW WE MET	WHAT I LIKE ABOUT HIM OR HER	WHY HE OR SHE IS IMPORTANT IN MY LIFE

LESSON 29
DON'T ASSUME

OBJECTIVE

By the end of the lesson, students will be able to:

- explain how perception and context influence what we think about a situation or behavior,
- determine potential meanings of various events, and
- demonstrate problem-solving skills.

GUIDING QUESTIONS FOR STUDENTS

- How do I solve a problem with my friends?
- How does perception and context influence my interpretation of the problem?

GUIDING PRINCIPLES

Problems can occur in any relationship. Many times it appears that there is no apparent reason for the problem. And sometimes we never find out the reason for the problem. In friendships, it is important that we develop problem-solving skills and not assume we know what our friends are thinking. Recognizing when we make an assumption is an important step in problem solving with our friends.

MATERIALS

- Handout 29.1: Assumptions
- Crayons, colored pencils, or other writing utensils for students
- Whiteboard, flipchart, or smart board for discussion

INTRODUCTION

Arrange desks in groups of 2–4. Introduce guiding principles and any necessary vocabulary. Give each student the handout.

ACTIVITY

- Introduce the concept of making assumptions and how initial situations can have many possible meanings. Ask students to brainstorm various events that could have multiple meanings. Ask students to provide examples of the assumptions people could make and possible actual meanings for the examples.

■ Discuss the worksheet responses as a large group.

■ Assign each group one of the example scenarios on Handout 29.1. Instruct the groups to determine what someone could do to avoid making assumptions and get to the "real" meaning of the situation.

■ Invite each group to role-play its solutions for the class.

DISCUSSION

Discuss how assumptions can impact friendships. Use the following discussion questions to aid the conversation:

■ Are most assumptions positive or negative?

■ How can you find out what your friend is thinking instead of making assumptions?

■ What do you think would happen if you didn't make assumptions? Would your friendship be stronger?

ASSESSMENT

Evaluate the students' responses based on appropriate standards.

Name: _____ Date: _____

ASSUMPTIONS

Directions: Complete based on the activity.

EVENT	POSSIBLE ASSUMPTIONS SOMEONE COULD MAKE	POSSIBLE MEANINGS FOR THE EVENT
Your friend sits in the back of the room rocking and singing a nursery rhyme.		
Two students begin to talk to each other in loud voices.		
A girl is sitting in the corner with a very sad look on her face.		
A teacher comes in after lunch and uses a loud voice to ask the students to sit down and take a quiz.		
Your mother comes in to the house and sighs deeply.		

LESSON 30
MY CHEER SQUAD

OBJECTIVE
By the end of the lesson, students will be able to:
- explain the importance of building connections with others, and
- identify personal support teams.

GUIDING QUESTION FOR STUDENTS
- Who can I turn to for support when things get difficult?

GUIDING PRINCIPLES
Another aspect of resiliency involves the ability to recognize your personal circle of support and accept help when offered. For many gifted individuals, leaning on a support network is paramount to admission of failure. It is important for gifted individuals to recognize their personal support teams and why these teams are so important for resiliency.

MATERIALS
- Handout 30.1: Network of Support Graphic Organizer
- Handout 30.2: My Cheer Squad
- Crayons, colored pencils, or other writing utensils for students
- Whiteboard, flipchart, or smart board for discussion

INTRODUCTION
Introduce guiding principles and vocabulary. Give each student the handouts.

ACTIVITY
- Discuss the importance of knowing who your support team is. Include examples from stories, movies, and/or pop culture.
- Ask students to brainstorm places people can find their support system. Instruct students to complete the graphic organizer.
- Instruct students to complete the My Cheer Squad handout by writing the names of their support team in the spaces provided. Use the information from the graphic organizer as needed. Decorate the handout as time permits.

DISCUSSION

Discuss how support teams can help you when times are difficult and during periods of success. Use the following discussion questions to aid the conversation:

- Why is it important to understand who your support team is?
- How has your support team helped you?
- How can you be supportive to someone else?

ASSESSMENT

Evaluate the students' projects based on appropriate standards.

NETWORK OF SUPPORT GRAPHIC ORGANIZER

Directions: Make a list of those people in your life who support you and who you feel safe with.

FAMILY MEMBERS	FRIENDS	OTHER PEOPLE I TRUST AND FEEL SAFE WITH

MY CHEER SQUAD

LESSON 31
DO YOU UNDERSTAND ME?

OBJECTIVE

By the end of the lesson, students will be able to:

- explain the importance of good communication skills, and
- identity the different aspects of communication.

GUIDING QUESTIONS FOR STUDENTS

- Do I know how to effectively communicate my needs and wants?
- Am I a good listener to others?

GUIDING PRINCIPLES

One of the cornerstones of building healthy connections to others is developing strong communication skills. Communication involves both speaking and listening skills. It is important to be able to effectively communicate ideas, as well as listen to the ideas coming from others. By developing critical speaking and listening skills, gifted individuals can enhance their relationships in all aspects of their lives.

MATERIALS

- Two pieces of drawing paper per group
- Crayons, colored pencils, or other writing utensils for students
- Whiteboard, flipchart, or smart board for discussion

INTRODUCTION

Arrange desks in groups of two, backs toward each other. Introduce guiding principles. Give each student two pieces of drawing paper.

ACTIVITY

- Ask each student to draw a picture of a monster. It can be any monster and can be decorated any way he or she wants. After a maximum of 5 minutes, instruct the students to get out a new piece of drawing paper.
- Ask one member of each student pair to verbally describe his or her drawing to the other student. Tell them to be careful not to show the drawing to the other student. The other student is to draw a monster based on the descrip-

tion provided by his or her partner. After 5 minutes, switch roles so that each student has the opportunity to both draw and describe his or her monster.

■ Once all drawings are complete, share the pair of drawings. Instruct students to look for similarities and differences.

DISCUSSION

Discuss the experience as it related to developing critical listening and speaking skills. Use the following discussion questions to aid the conversation:

■ What was the most difficult aspect of the experience?
■ Did your opinions of your communication skills change at all? How?
■ How can you strengthen your verbal skills? Your listening skills?
■ What did you learn?

ASSESSMENT

Evaluate the students' responses based on appropriate standards.

LESSON 32
COMMUNICATION ROADBLOCKS

OBJECTIVE

By the end of the lesson, students will be able to:

- identify and define communication roadblocks,
- discuss the difference between effective and ineffective communication, and
- describe how listener response impacts the speaker.

GUIDING QUESTION FOR STUDENTS

- How can I effectively listen and communicate with others?

GUIDING PRINCIPLES

Effective communication requires both clear communication from the speaker and good listening skills. Sometimes the way a listener reacts to the speaker can stop effective communication from happening. Being able to identify various roadblocks and the impact of these on communication is an essential step toward becoming a good listener and developing effective communication techniques.

MATERIALS

- Crayons, colored pencils, or other writing utensils for students
- Whiteboard, flipchart, or smart board for discussion

INTRODUCTION

Introduce guiding principles and vocabulary.

ACTIVITY

- The following roadblocks should be listed on the board:
  - *language*: use of jargon or unfamiliar words
  - *emotional*: discussing topics that are of a highly emotional nature
  - *internal*: use of sarcasm, put-downs, yelling or whining, and other threatening forms of communication
  - *perception*: differences in point of view and perception of the topic
  - *nonverbal communication*: "closed" body language and other nonverbal communication that shuts down the communication

■ Define the above roadblocks. Demonstrate an example of each one.

■ Ask students to pick a partner and decide who is the speaker and who is the listener. Role-play each of the communication roadblocks. When each of the roadblocks is finished, switch roles until every student has been both the speaker and the listener.

DISCUSSION

Discuss how it felt to be the speaker faced with the various roadblocks. Use the following discussion questions to aid the conversation:

■ How did the roadblocks prevent effective communication?

■ Which roadblock made the speaker feel the worst? Which roadblock made the listener feel the worst?

■ What did you learn from the experience?

ASSESSMENT

Evaluate the students' responses based on appropriate standards.

LESSON 33
LEARN TO LISTEN

OBJECTIVE

By the end of the lesson, students will be able to:

- explain what it means to listen, and
- develop 1–3 strategies to improve listening skills.

GUIDING QUESTIONS FOR STUDENTS

- What does it mean to be a good listener?
- How can I improve my listening skills?

GUIDING PRINCIPLES

One of the most important aspects of strong communication skills is the art of listening. In today's world of increasing noise, listening and good communication skills are decreasing. Developing the art of listening is a necessary tool to both understanding and connecting.

MATERIALS

- Handout 33.1: TED Talk Reflection
- Equipment and ability to show a TED talk to the class
- Poster paper
- Crayons, colored pencils, or other writing utensils for students
- Whiteboard, flipchart, or smart board for discussion

INTRODUCTION

Introduce guiding principles. Give each student the handout.

ACTIVITY

- Show the TED talk video (located at http://www.ted.com/talks/julian_treasure_5_ways_to_listen_better) to the group. As with any link, please watch the video prior to using it with the class.
- Ask students to complete the TED Talk Reflection (Handout 33.1).
- Ask students provide examples of ways to improve listening skills.
- Instruct table groups to pick one strategy and make a "how-to" poster. (*Note.* Videos or vlogs can also be made instead of the poster.)

DISCUSSION

Discuss the importance of developing strong listening skills. Use the following discussion questions to aid the conversation:

- Why is listening more difficult now?
- Do you agree with the TED talk presenter? Why or why not?
- Do you think it is important for schools to teaching conscious listening skills?
- What is one way these skills can be taught?

ASSESSMENT

Evaluate the students' projects and responses based on appropriate standards.

TED TALK REFLECTION

1. Topic: _____

2. Two things I found most interesting:

   _____

   _____

3. Something I didn't know before:

   _____

   _____

4. How I will use this information:

   _____

   _____

LESSON 34
ATTRIBUTES OF A LEADER

OBJECTIVE

By the end of the lesson, students will be able to:

- identify the specific qualities of leadership,
- explain the meaning of leadership, and
- identify personal leadership qualities.

GUIDING QUESTION FOR STUDENTS

- What are the specific traits of an effective leader?

GUIDING PRINCIPLES

Successful individuals often demonstrate the qualities of leadership throughout their lives. Leaders are not always born; sometimes they are created by developing specific traits. Knowing what these traits are and how to use them in a variety of situations is the key to developing personal leadership skills.

MATERIALS

- 3 x 5 cards
- Crayons, colored pencils, or other writing utensils for students
- Whiteboard, flipchart, or smart board for discussion

INTRODUCTION

Arrange desks into groups of 3–4. Introduce guiding principles and vocabulary. Provide each student with five 3 x 5 cards.

ACTIVITY

- Discuss the meaning of leadership. Invite students to think of examples of leaders in history.
- Ask students to write down five qualities they think are important in leadership.
- Working in groups, ask each group to pick five total traits from the ones written by the students. Invite each group to write its answers on the large paper,

one group at a time. No traits can be duplicated—if a group sees its answer(s) already written, it must come up with a new trait.

- Working in groups, ask groups to pick five traits and develop a PowerPoint explaining the traits. (*Note.* Students can develop a comic strip as an alternative assignment.)

DISCUSSION

Discuss the specific leadership traits and the importance of developing these traits. Use the following discussion questions to aid the conversation:

- What traits have you begun to develop already? Which ones give you the most trouble?
- Do you see a connection between these traits and emotional intelligence factors? What is it?
- What trait seems most important to you and why?

ASSESSMENT

Evaluate the students' projects based on appropriate standards.

LESSON 35
THE SUM OF ITS PARTS

OBJECTIVE

By the end of the lesson, students will be able to:
- explain the benefits and drawbacks of collaboration, and
- identify skills needed for effective collaboration.

GUIDING QUESTION FOR STUDENTS

- Why is collaboration considered a necessary skill in today's world?

GUIDING PRINCIPLES

Collaboration is one of the most important skills according to today's business leaders. However, collaboration is not without its drawbacks. Understanding both the benefits and drawbacks to collaboration is necessary in order to develop and utilize both collaboration and creative thinking in school and the workplace.

MATERIALS

- Handout 35.1: Group Collaboration Cards
- Crayons, colored pencils, or other writing utensils for students
- Whiteboard, flipchart, or smart board for discussion

INTRODUCTION

Arrange desks in groups of 4–5. Introduce guiding principles and cooperative group roles. Provide each student with the handout.

ACTIVITY

- Give one member of each group the Facilitator role. Remind them that the Facilitator is responsible for assigning the rest of the roles. Instruct each group to develop a short (5-minute max) lesson on the importance of collaboration, with each member of the group fulfilling his or her assigned role.
- Ask each group to present its lesson to the class.
- As one group performs, ask the other groups to watch and find 1–2 things they learned from the experience.

DISCUSSION

Discuss collaboration as a concept. Be sure to include a discussion of the pros and cons of working as a team. Use the following discussion questions to aid the conversation:

- Why is collaboration considered a necessary skill in the workforce?
- What are the specific drawbacks to collaboration and how can they be overcome?
- What are the traits necessary for collaboration? Which traits do you currently demonstrate?

ASSESSMENT

Evaluate the students' projects based on appropriate standards.

GROUP COLLABORATION CARDS

Facilitator: Decides who does what in the group, keeps the group on track.	**Recorder:** Keeps notes about the activities of the group.
Timekeeper: Makes sure the group stays on track and manages time.	**Materials coordinator:** Makes sure the group has what it needs for completion of the task.

CHAPTER 9

Unit V
Cultivating Your Talents and Passions

No conversation about guiding gifted children would be complete without a discussion of talent development. Researchers have pointed to the need to assist gifted children in self-exploration of their individual learning styles and interests, as well as future career opportunities related to their interest areas (Jung, 2012). Additionally, gifted students benefit from increased opportunities for creative expressions, leadership development, and positive psychology models of support (Renzulli, 2009, 2012; Stewart, 2007; Wilcox, 2013). Talent development can encourage and nurture high-potential children, reducing declining performance that can happen in secondary education (Siegle, 2013; Stewart, 2007). This is probably why the National Association of Gifted Children (2010) has included talent development and career exploration among its list of standards.

The purpose of this unit is to support talents and interest exploration, encourage development, and nurture creative thinking and career guidance. Using a combination of interest inventories, career research exercises, creative problem solving, and social compentence development, the following lessons are designed to foster increased engagement and meaning for gifted students (Bisland, 2004; Jung, 2014; Maxwell, 2007). This, in turn, can improve student outcomes during their K–12 educational years (Jung, 2013; Kong, 2013; Siegle, 2013) and beyond.

UNIT OVERVIEW

The 10 lessons in this unit cover four broad skill areas as follows:

- *Exploring learning styles and developing creativity* (Lessons 36–38): The lessons in this section focus on understanding personal learning styles and interests from multiple constructs and connecting the information to future career goals. An exploration of creative problem solving is also included.

■ *Discovering your talents and interests* (Lessons 39–41): These lessons focus on identifying strengths, cultivating confidence, and discovering new interest areas as they related to potential career aspirations.

■ *Goal setting and decision making* (Lessons 42–43): One of the cornerstones skills that can be developed alongside talent development is goal-setting. The two lessons in this section focus on the components of goal-setting and decision-making skills.

■ *Career and life guidance* (Lessons 44–45): The unit ends with planning exercises that focus on connecting education to career exploration and life. These lessons emphasize the values of living from a purpose-driven point of view.

As with the previous units, the overall value of the lessons is enhanced through diversity. In the case of talent development, enrichment can be added through the inclusion of speakers and opportunities for students to find mentors in their fields of interest. Connecting current educational goals to future aspirations is vital for gifted children in order to develop a stronger sense of meaning and social competence (Renzulli, 2009; Siegle, 2013).

EXTENSION OPPORTUNITIES

Some potential extension activities that can build on the lessons in this unit include the following:

■ Set up career walks with experts from the community or through online study.

■ Offer out-of-class experiences through TED and other programming.

■ Day in which students become an "expert-for-a-day" on areas of talent or interest.

■ Develop a resource book for out-of-classroom opportunities.

■ Write an autobiography.

LESSON 36
MANY WAYS TO LEARN

OBJECTIVE

By the end of the lesson, students will be able to:
- differentiate between Gardner's different learning styles as indicated by multiple intelligences,
- identify personal strengths and weaknesses in learning styles, and
- explain how multiple intelligences factor into job interests and daily performance.

GUIDING QUESTION FOR STUDENTS

- What multiple intelligences factor into my learning style preferences?

GUIDING PRINCIPLES

For the past several decades, educators have used Gardner's theory of multiple intelligences as a guiding principle to explain learning styles. Although there is little research to support the idea of distinct intelligences, using Gardner's theory to examine personal learning styles and learning preferences can help students begin to identify potential careers. For gifted individuals, this exploration into learning styles and possible career tracks should begin at a young age in order to provide increased meaning to daily school experiences.

MATERIALS

- Handout 36.1: Multiple Intelligences (MI)
- Computer with Internet access
- Crayons, colored pencils, or other writing utensils for students
- Whiteboard, flipchart, or smart board for discussion

INTRODUCTION

Introduce guiding principles and any needed vocabulary. Provide each student with a computer and Internet access. Provide students with the handout.

ACTIVITY

- Discuss each of Gardner's multiple intelligences, providing examples of each domain. Ask students to brainstorm additional examples for each domain. Instruct students to complete Section 1 of the worksheet.
- Visit the following website and ask students to take the multiple intelligences assessment: http://www.edutopia.org/multiple-intelligences-assessment. Please preview all sites prior to allowing student access.
- Instruct students to input their results on the worksheet.
- Help students to complete the rest of Section 1 of the worksheet.

DISCUSSION

Discuss the role of multiple intelligences in career planning and talent development. Use the following discussion questions to aid the conversation:

- Do you think it is important to understand your learning styles or multiple intelligences? Why or why not?
- Does this information help with career planning? How?

ASSESSMENT

Instruct students to write a short paragraph in Section 2 of the handout explaining the importance of understanding their personal learning styles. Evaluate the students' projects based on appropriate standards.

Name: _____ Date: _____

MULTIPLE INTELLIGENCES (MI)

SECTION 1: A LOOK AT MI

Directions: Complete column A based on the class discussion. After completing the quiz, complete columns B and C.

LEARNING STYLE	A. DEFINITION	B. QUIZ RESULTS	C. HOW DO YOU SHOW THIS?
Linguistic/Verbal			
Logical/ Mathematical			
Visual/Spatial			
Intrapersonal			
Interpersonal			
Musical			
Bodily/ Kinesthetic			
Naturalistic			

SECTION 2

Directions: Use the box below to write a paragraph explaining the importance of understanding your learning preferences.

LESSON 37
MY CHARACTER AND QUALITIES INVENTORY

OBJECTIVE

By the end of the lesson, students will be able to:

* identify career areas best suited to their self-identified character traits,
* identify 3–5 careers within each character trait, and
* choose 1–3 potential careers.

GUIDING QUESTIONS FOR STUDENTS

* What are my interests, strengths, and needs as a gifted student?
* How do my character strengths inform my potential career choices?

GUIDING PRINCIPLES

Successful people who enjoy their jobs have careers that suit their unique personalities. Their career choices enable them to use their skills and work in an environment that suits their temperament, passions, skills, and purpose. Identifying your career personality is one way to begin to find job choices that may bring you the most satisfaction.

MATERIALS

* Handout 37.1: Skills/Careers
* Computer with Internet access
* Crayons, colored pencils, or other writing utensils for students
* Whiteboard, flipchart, or smart board for discussion

INTRODUCTION

Introduce guiding principles and any needed vocabulary. Provide each student with a computer and Internet access. Provide students with the worksheet.

ACTIVITY

* Discuss character traits like those found on the word bank in Lesson 45 (see page 176). Ask students to think about their top five traits and write them on the worksheet.

▓ Visit the following website and ask students to take the character self-assessment using the five traits highlighted previously, as well any additional areas of strength: http://www.educationplanner.org/students/self-assessments/character.shtml. Please preview all sites prior to allowing student access.

▓ Using the worksheet, ask students to complete columns B and C based on their results.

▓ Ask students to share their results with a partner.

DISCUSSION

Discuss the role of work environment, temperament, interests, and skills in career planning and talent development. Use the following discussion questions to aid the conversation:

▓ What are the most important factors to consider when choosing potential careers?

▓ Do you agree with the assessment results? Why or why not?

▓ Did you learn anything new about yourself through this process?

ASSESSMENT

Evaluate the students' discussions based on appropriate standards.

SKILLS/CAREERS

Directions: Complete column A based on the class discussion. After completing the quiz, complete columns B and C.

A. CHARACTER TRAIT	B. DEFINITION (FROM WEBSITE)	C. POTENTIAL CAREERS/JOBS (FROM WEBSITE)

Write 1–3 potential career choices and why they are of interest to you.

_____

_____

_____

_____

_____

_____

_____

_____

_____

LESSON 38
DIVERGENCE

OBJECTIVE

By the end of the lesson, students will be able to:
- use the SCAMPER tool for creative exploration,
- demonstrate divergent and creative thinking skills, and
- articulate the benefits of creative problem solving.

GUIDING QUESTION FOR STUDENTS

- How can I develop my own creative problem solving skills?

GUIDING PRINCIPLES

The need for creative problem solving in the professional fields is well known. However, developing creativity is something absent in many academic arenas. The SCAMPER method developed by Bob Eberle is one way to develop creativity. Using these principles, gifted children can delve deeper into their creative selves, regardless of their learning and skill preferences. This creative approach to thinking can then be generalized for use in any future academic or career path whenever creative problem solving skills are needed.

MATERIALS

- Handout 38.1: SCAMPER Graphic Organizer
- Miscellaneous classroom items (i.e., ruler, stapler, pipe cleaner, penny or other change, etc.)
- Crayons, colored pencils, or other writing utensils for students
- Whiteboard, flipchart, or smart board for discussion

INTRODUCTION

Arrange the desks into groups of 2–4. Introduce guiding principles and any required vocabulary. Provide each student with the handout. Provide each table group with a common classroom or household item.

ACTIVITY

- Discuss creativity and the SCAMPER method. Using one of the common objects for an example, invite students to problem solve new, innovative ways to use the object. Write student examples on the board or smart board.
- Ask table groups to use the other provided items and problem solve new and innovative ways to use each one. They should complete the graphic organizer with the information provided by the group.

DISCUSSION

Discuss the pros and cons of the SCAMPER method of problem solving. Use the following discussion questions to aid the conversation:

- Was this method helpful for you? In what way?
- How can you apply this method in the classroom? In everyday life?
- What is your take-away message from this experience?

ASSESSMENT

Evaluate the students' responses and efforts based on appropriate standards.

Name: _____ Date: _____

SCAMPER GRAPHIC ORGANIZER

Directions: Using the SCAMPER method, complete the table as a small group using the items provided.

	ITEM # 1	ITEM #2	ITEM #3
Substitute: What can be used instead?			
Combine: What things, processes, etc., can be combined?			
Adapt: What can change?			
Modify: Can it be distorted into another use/meaning?			
Put to Other Uses: What else can it be used for?			
Eliminate: What can you reduce or eliminate?			
Rearrange: What can you replace, change, or rework?			

LESSON 39
DO WHAT YOU LOVE

OBJECTIVE

By the end of the lesson, students will be able to:

■ identify their passions and interests,

■ identify careers related to their passions and interests, and

■ develop a goal related to their passions and interests.

GUIDING QUESTIONS FOR STUDENTS

■ What am I most passionate about?

■ What careers match my passions and interests?

GUIDING PRINCIPLES

Successful people have many traits in common, including matching their chosen career with their interests and passions. However, it is not always simple to discover what your passions actually are. This is particularly true with gifted individuals who often have many interests. In addition to discovering your interests, it is also important to see the connection between interests and future career aspirations. This connection can guide the educational process and provide gifted individuals with the motivation they may need.

MATERIALS

■ Handout 39.1: Passions

■ Blank poster board

■ Magazine clippings and/or access to Internet for pictures

■ Crayons, colored pencils, or other writing utensils for students

■ Whiteboard, flipchart, or smart board for discussion

INTRODUCTION

Arrange tables in groups of 2–4. Introduce the idea of "passions," the guiding principles, and any required vocabulary. Give each student the handout and a piece of poster board. Have students write their name in the center of the poster board. (*Note.* The project portion of the lesson can be adapted for digital completion, making a digital vision board instead of a physical one. Websites like Pinterest, PicMonkey, as well as apps including Jack Canfield's Success Vision Board, iWish, and Vision Cooker are great options to use.)

ACTIVITY

- Discuss the concept of interests and passions. Use examples from successful entrepreneurs like Steve Jobs, Walt Disney, and Mark Zuckerberg. Invite students to come up with their own examples.
- Discuss subject areas people can study in school. Ask table groups to discuss how various subject areas can be used in passion areas using the examples already discussed in class to complete Section 1 of the handout.
- Invite students to brainstorm their own, individual lists of passions. Write the list on Section 2 of the handout.
- Ask students to connect their list of passions to curricular areas and complete Section 2 of the handout.

DISCUSSION

Discuss the handout as a large group. Focus on how curriculum areas can relate to passions. Use the following discussion questions to aid the conversation:

- What curricular areas can help you with your areas of interest?
- Why is it important to not only know your passions, but also how education can support your passions?
- Do you think it is better to begin focusing on your passions at a younger age? Why or why not?

ASSESSMENT

Instruct students to create a vision board with the poster paper provided. They should use magazine clippings or images from the Internet to create a vision board of their passions and ways they can be involved. Digital vision boards can also be created. Evaluate the students' projects based on appropriate standards.

PASSIONS

SECTION 1: EXAMPLES OF PASSIONS AND SCHOOL/SKILLS

Directions: Complete each column based on the small-group discussion.

PASSIONS (SOCIAL/PERSONAL ISSUES THAT EVOKE STRONG OPINIONS/EMOTIONS)	SCHOOL SUBJECTS/SKILLS (SKILL AREAS THAT CAN HELP A PERSON TAKE ACTION WITH HIS OR HER PASSION)	ACTIONS (THINGS A PERSON CAN DO TO SUPPORT HIS OR HER PASSION AREAS)
Global warming	Science, communication, speech/debate, writing	Start a conservation blog, implement an awareness campaign, write legislators about the issues

SECTION 2: MY PASSIONS

Directions: Now fill out each column based on *your* passions.

PASSIONS (SOCIAL/PERSONAL ISSUES THAT EVOKE STRONG OPINIONS/EMOTIONS IN YOU)	SCHOOL SUBJECTS/SKILLS (SKILL AREAS THAT CAN HELP YOU TAKE ACTION WITH YOUR PASSION)	ACTIONS (THINGS YOU CAN DO TO SUPPORT YOUR PASSION AREAS)
Global warming	Science, communication, speech/debate, writing	Start a conservation blog, implement an awareness campaign, write legislators about the issues

LESSON 40
I AM ENOUGH

OBJECTIVE

By the end of the lesson, students will be able to:

- identify their strengths, weaknesses, and quirks;
- identify limiting thoughts; and
- develop a self-acceptance plan of action.

GUIDING QUESTION FOR STUDENTS

- What does it mean to accept myself as I am?

GUIDING PRINCIPLES

Self-acceptance is a key component of self-esteem and predictor of future happiness. For gifted individuals, perfectionism and faulty thinking can often get in the way of the development of healthy self-acceptance. It is important for gifted individuals to recognize the many facets of themselves, including strengths, weaknesses, quirks, and things they'd like to change in order to develop a healthy self-acceptance.

MATERIALS

- Handout 40.1: Who Am I?
- Three large pieces of paper hung around the room, labeled "strengths," "weaknesses," and "quirks"
- Crayons, colored pencils, or other writing utensils for students
- Whiteboard, flipchart, or smart board for discussion

INTRODUCTION

Introduce guiding principles and any needed vocabulary. Give each student the worksheet.

ACTIVITY

- Instruct students to complete Section 1 of Handout 40.1.
- Pair students into groups of two and ask the students to interview each other, using the questions on Section 2 of the worksheet.

- Using the information from the interview, ask students to walk around the room and list a few of their strengths, weaknesses, and quirks on the sheets provided. No names should be used.
- Ask the students to complete the self-reflection questions (Section 3) of the handout.

DISCUSSION

As a group, discuss how everyone is a combination of many attributes. Everyone has things he or she would like to change and things he or she admires about him- or herself. Discuss what self-acceptance is and how to focus on the positive, realistic strengths. Use the following discussion questions to aid the conversation:

- What are the strengths, weaknesses, and quirks you discovered?
- Did you learn anything new about your classmates?
- How can you achieve a positive self-acceptance?

ASSESSMENT

Instruct students to write a brief class biography, indicating the strengths, weaknesses, and quirks of the group. End the biography with a positive statement of acceptance. Evaluate the students' work based on appropriate standards.

WHO AM I?

SECTION 1: INTERVIEW PREP

Directions: Take a moment to think about each question and then answer as fully as you can.

1. What do you care deeply about (e.g., animals, family, helping others, etc.)?

_____

_____

_____

_____

2. What makes you angry and causes a strong emotional reaction from you (e.g., discrimination, global warming, poverty, etc.)?

_____

_____

_____

_____

3. If you could only do or be 10 things in your lifetime, what would they be?

_____

_____

_____

_____

4. Now, take the list above and limit it to five. What are the five things?

_____

_____

_____

_____

5. List three strengths, three weaknesses, and three quirks or things that make you unique in some way.

_____

_____

_____

_____

SECTION 2: INTERVIEW QUESTIONS

Directions: Ask the following questions to a partner and fill in their responses below.

1. Tell me three strengths, three weaknesses, and three quirks about you.

_____

_____

_____

_____

2. What would you like to be known for?

_____

_____

_____

_____

3. Tell me something about you that few other people know.

_____

_____

_____

_____

4. If you could do or be anything, what would it be?

_____

_____

_____

_____

5. What are the 1–2 obstacles standing in the way of achieving your dreams?

_____

_____

_____

_____

SECTION 3: SELF-REFLECTION

Directions: Read and answer the questions below:

1. What strengths are you most proud of and why?

_____

_____

_____

_____

2. What weaknesses are most troubling to you and why?

_____

_____

_____

_____

3. What did you learn from this experience?

_____

_____

_____

_____

LESSON 41
STRENGTHENING MY WEAKNESSES

OBJECTIVE

By the end of the lesson, students will be able to:

- identify personal strengths and weakness,
- evaluate perceived and/or actual weaknesses, and
- develop an action plan for perceived and/or actual weaknesses.

GUIDING QUESTIONS FOR THE STUDENTS

- Are my perceptions regarding my weaknesses accurate?
- Can I strengthen or overcome my weaknesses?

GUIDING PRINCIPLES

No one is perfect, despite the gifted individual's efforts to be so. Discovering and accepting personal weaknesses can be difficult for gifted individuals. Sometimes behaviors that are perceived as weaknesses are really strengths we've chosen to ignore. It is important to accurately understand our weaknesses and manage the impact they have in our lives. Successful people achieve their dreams not from a place of perfection, but from acceptance of everything that they are—their personal strengths and weaknesses.

MATERIALS

- Handout 40.1: Who Am I?, completed
- Handout 41.1: All of Me Graphic Organizer
- Materials to make a kaleidoscope. Refer to your favorite DIY site (such as https://diy.org/skills/toymaker/challenges/773/build-a-kaleidoscope) for more information.
- Crayons, colored pencils, or other writing utensils for students
- Whiteboard, flipchart, or smart board for discussion

INTRODUCTION

Introduce guiding principles and any required vocabulary. Give each student his or her completed version of Handout 40.1 and the blank Handout 41.1.

ACTIVITY

- Discuss how some weaknesses are strengths in disguise. Invite students to provide examples.
- Ask students to refer to Handout 40.1. If they have not completed Sections 1 and 3, instruct them to do so now.
- Based on the information in the worksheet, instruct students to complete the graphic organizer in Handout 41.1. Ask students which weaknesses listed may be strengths in disguise and make a list of these traits or behaviors.
- Ask students to brainstorm ways to improve weaknesses.
- Create a kaleidoscope to demonstrate how objects shift and change based on perspective.

DISCUSSION

Discuss strengths and weaknesses. Use the following discussion questions to aid the conversation:

- Are some of your personal weaknesses strengths in disguise? How do you know?
- What can you do to turn a weakness into a strength?
- What did building a kaleidoscope teach you?
- Why is it important to acknowledge weaknesses and work on strengthening them?

ASSESSMENT

Evaluate the students' responses based on appropriate standards.

ALL OF ME GRAPHIC ORGANIZER

Directions: Using the information from Handout 40.1, write down your perceived weaknesses in the spots provided. What proof do you have that the habit/trait or skill is actually a weakness? Write that in the appropriate column. Complete the rest as the activity continues.

PERCEIVED WEAKNESS	PROOF	STRENGTH IN DISGUISE?	WHAT YOU CAN DO TO STRENGTHEN IT
Math	I never like doing math. I dread going to my math class. If it were a strength of mine, I think I would like the subject.	I earn A's on my tests and understand the material in class. Yes, it is a strength.	I need to consider that maybe I am good at math, maybe there is something related to math that I will like.

Now, take a moment and write a few words or sentences to describe what you learned about yourself.

_____

_____

_____

What did the kaleidoscope activity teach you?

_____

_____

_____

LESSON 42
PLAN AHEAD

OBJECTIVE

By the end of the lesson, students will be able to:

- identify the essential components of goal setting,
- explain the purpose of having goals, and
- develop one goal and its steps.

GUIDING QUESTION FOR STUDENTS

- Why is goal setting important?

GUIDING PRINCIPLES

Success rarely happens by accident. It is the byproduct of hard work, courage, and goal setting. Learning how to write an effective goal is a necessary habit to develop for success. Understanding the components of goal setting, including defining the goal in specific, measurable terms, clarifying your objectives, and creating deadlines, will give you the foundation needed to move you in the direction of your goals and dreams.

MATERIALS

- Handout 42.1: Goal-Setting
- Whiteboard, flipchart, or smart board for discussion

INTRODUCTION

Introduce guiding principles. Give each student the worksheet.

ACTIVITY

- Instruct students to find the treasure in the class. Tell them that the only way to find it is to be very quiet and follow the rules exactly. Say nothing else. If a question is asked, remind the students to be quiet and follow the rules exactly. Say nothing else. Your students will likely wait for more instructions, but say nothing. After a while, ask the students what the problem was with the instructions (there are no instructions, just as there is no treasure). Discuss the need to know where you are, where you need to go, and steps to get there.

- Discuss the principles of goal setting. Include the components as listed on the worksheet.
- Instruct students to write one goal with its steps as indicated on the goal worksheet. This goal should relate to an area of interest or talent.

DISCUSSION

Discuss the importance of setting specific goals. Use the following discussion questions to aid the conversation:

- Why is it important to be specific in your goal?
- Why should goals be measurable?
- Are the steps really that important to achieving the goal? Why or why not?

ASSESSMENT

Evaluate the students' participation based on appropriate standards.

Name:_____ Date: _____

GOAL-SETTING

Directions: Set one goal for yourself related to an interest or talent area. These should be short term and must include every component. Examples are included in italics.

STEPS	STATEMENT
Time frame for goal completion	By next week
What will you do? Be specific.	I will inquire about summer programs at my local art studio.
How will you do it?	I will call the studio directly.
If that doesn't work, what else can you do?	I can e-mail them or ask my parents to drive me to the studio to ask them in person.
Put it all together	By next week, I will inquire about summer programs at my local art studio by calling the studio. If that does not work, I can e-mail them or ask my parents to drive me to the studio.

LESSON 43
SO MANY CHOICES

OBJECTIVE

By the end of the lesson, students will be able to:

- connect interests to education and career choices,
- identify 1–3 potential careers, and
- develop potential paths for achieving their career choices.

GUIDING QUESTIONS FOR STUDENTS

- How do my specific interests and passions relate to academic courses and future careers?
- What kinds of paths lead to my future career choices?

GUIDING PRINCIPLES

Success is more than having passions and interests. It is connecting those passions to a career path. It is also developing the skills necessary to develop an action plan that will lead a person from simply having a dream to achieving it. Understanding how various academic studies can feed an individual's passions and crafting a path is a necessary part of achieving one's goals.

MATERIALS

- Handout 43.1: My Interests
- Handout 43.2: Many Choices Graphic Organizer
- Crayons, colored pencils, or other writing utensils for students
- Whiteboard, flipchart, or smart board for discussion

INTRODUCTION

Discuss the connection between interests, school, and potential careers. Introduce guiding principles and any necessary vocabulary. Provide the handouts to each student.

ACTIVITY

- List academic subject areas on the board or overhead. Refer to Handout 43.1. Invite students to add to the list of subject areas as needed.

- Instruct students to brainstorm potential careers related to each academic subject area. Some careers may fit in more than one area.
- Instruct students to complete Handout 43.1.
- Using the information on the handout, ask students to pick up to three potential career areas. Ask students to write their career choices in the appropriate spaces on the graphic organizer (Handout 43.2). Instruct students to complete the graphic organizer, listing the steps needed to reach the career goal. Provide examples as necessary to assist the students.
- Students may decorate the graphic organizer if there is time.

DISCUSSION

Discuss the importance of connecting academic courses, interests, and future career plans. Use the following discussion questions to aid the conversation:

- How did your ideas about careers change as you began to connect academic course work and interests?
- What did you learn from the graphic organizer?
- How can you connect your current school experiences to your future goals?

ASSESSMENT

Instruct students to write a paragraph connecting passions, academic subject preferences, and future career choices. The paragraph should defend their specific career choices related to the subject preferences and specific interests or passions. Evaluate the students' projects based on appropriate standards.

MY INTERESTS

SECTION 1: LINKING INTERESTS TO CAREERS

Directions: Look at the academic subject and/or skill areas listed. Brainstorm potential careers related to each subject area. The first one has been completed for you. Add to it and then complete the rest.

ACADEMIC SUBJECT AREA	POTENTIAL CAREERS/JOBS
Performing arts	Dancer Musician Composer Audio engineer
Visual arts	
English	
Math	
Science	
Social Studies	
Writing	
Speech/Debate	
Other:	

SECTION 2: CAREER CONNECTIONS

Directions: Pick 3–5 potential career choices. Brainstorm ways for you to achieve your career goal, including what kinds of classes you could take.

CAREER CHOICE	PATHWAY
Author	Take writing classes Start a blog Investigate schools for writing Volunteer at the paper Participate in NaNoWriMo

MANY CHOICES GRAPHIC ORGANIZER

Directions: Write your career goal on the top step. Write an action to get your toward that goal on each step from the bottom to the top.

GOAL

LESSON 44
MY PATH

OBJECTIVE

By the end of the lesson, students will be able to:
- explain their long-term educational and career goals,
- identify short-term goals needed to achieve their long-term goals, and
- identify skill areas that need to be developed in order to reach their goals.

GUIDING QUESTION FOR STUDENTS

- What are my long-term goals for my education and my career?

GUIDING PRINCIPLES

Developing long-range goals is often as important as short-term goals. These long-term goals can provide a map guiding us in the direction of our dreams. Gifted individuals benefit from talent development far earlier than previously understood. Developing long-term goals can often engage the gifted individual in their education, preventing the burnout or boredom that typically accompanies K–12 education for gifted individuals.

MATERIALS

- Handout 44.1: My Path Graphic Organizer
- Handout 44.2: My Path Map
- Computer availability to do an Internet search of careers of interest and potential educational paths
- Crayons, colored pencils, or other writing utensils for students
- Whiteboard, flipchart, or smart board for discussion

INTRODUCTION

Introduce guiding principles. Give each student the handouts.

ACTIVITY

- Discuss the purpose of setting long-term goals. Ask each student to brainstorm one career goal and one educational goal.

- Instruct students to research their chosen career and potential educational needs related to that career. Provide examples if needed.
- Ask students to complete the map based on the graphic organizer. Students may decorate the map if time permits.

DISCUSSION

Discuss the importance of having long-term goals and at least one potential plan to achieve the goals. Discuss the importance of talent development at an early age. Be sure to discuss the need for flexibility with long-term planning. Use the following discussion questions to aid the conversation:

- How can talent development encourage you now and later in school?
- Is it important to connect current learning with your career goals? Why or why not?
- What is the benefit to long-range planning?

ASSESSMENT

Evaluate the students' projects based on appropriate standards.

MY PATH GRAPHIC ORGANIZER

SECTION 1: LONG-TERM GOALS

Directions: Set one educational goal and one career goal. These are long-term goals, meaning you are not planning to achieve them for several years.

GOAL	PLAN	NEEDS
Educational goal #1: Learn how to create digital environments for video games.	• Contact CG schools and inquire about classes. • Write a letter/e-mail to someone who works in game design and ask how to get started. • Read about game design and creating digital environments.	• Information about gaming careers • The names of people in the industry • Access to computer technology
Educational goal:		
Career goal:		

SECTION 2: CAREER CONNECTIONS

Directions: Research the educational and skill requirements for your career interests. Complete the questions below.

1. What level of education is required for your career areas? Would increased education benefit you in the field in some way? What majors are typical for your chosen career goals?

   _____

   _____

   _____

2. What skills are required in your chosen interest/career areas? How can you acquire them? Are there any barriers you may encounter in acquiring these skills? How can you overcome them?

   _____

   _____

   _____

3. Set one educational and one career goal. These are long-term goals, meaning you are not planning to achieve them for several years.

   _____

   _____

   _____

Name: _____ Date: _____

MY PATH MAP

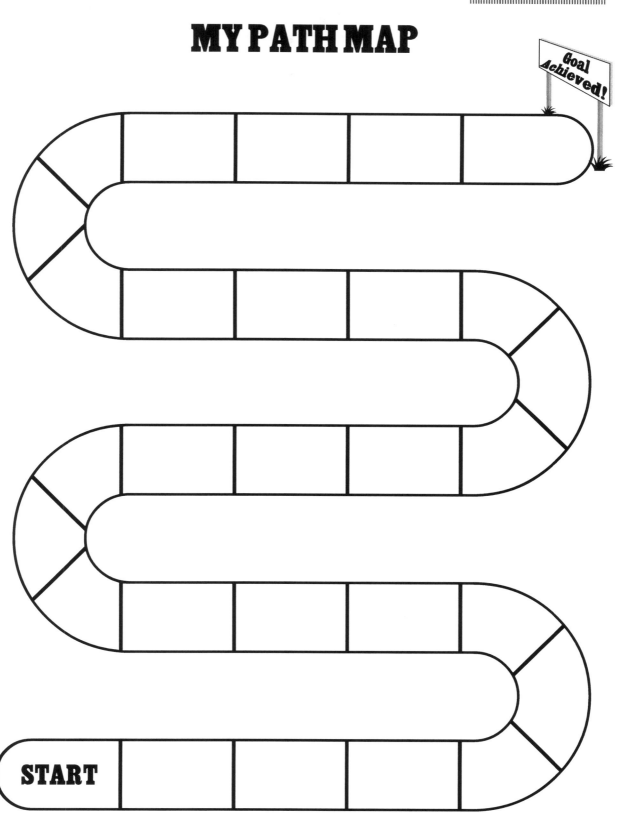

Goal Achieved!

START

LESSON 45
MISSION POSSIBLE

OBJECTIVE

By the end of the lesson, students will be able to:

- identify their values, skills, and talents;
- understand the value and purpose of a personal mission statement; and
- write a personal mission statement that describes their main motivations and purpose in life.

GUIDING QUESTIONS FOR STUDENTS

- What are my core values, my passions, and my talents?
- How can these attributes guide the direction of my life?
- What is my overall purpose?

GUIDING PRINCIPLES

- Gifted individuals benefit from deep self-analysis and an understanding of their purpose in life.
- Early talent development can reduce the potential for existential depression.

MATERIALS

- Ziploc or paper bags filled with the words from the supplied word bank—one bag for each: talents, values, passions
- Handout 45.1: Word Bank
- Handout 45.2: Mission Possible Graphic Organizer
- Crayons, colored pencils, or other writing utensils for students
- Whiteboard, flipchart, or smart board for discussion

INTRODUCTION

Arrange desks into groups of 2–4. Provide each table group with a bag of words. Give each student a graphic organizer. Introduce guiding principles and necessary vocabulary.

ACTIVITY

- Instruct students to take 5–10 words from each of the bags for values, talents, and passions.
- Using the graphic organizer, ask students to pick five words from each category and use them to complete the first section of the organizer.
- As the students to look over the list and identify patterns. Students may do this individually or in collaboration with their table group.
- Complete the rest of the graphic organizer, finishing with a personal mission statement. Ask table groups to share their statements with each other.

DISCUSSION

Discuss the purpose of a mission statement. Use the following discussion questions to aid the conversation:

- Why is it important to have a sense of purpose in life?
- What can happen when you are unclear of your purpose?
- What types of things can influence your purpose and your mission statement?

ASSESSMENT

Evaluate the students' projects based on appropriate standards.

WORD BANK

Directions: For each list of words, make cards and place in a paper bag (one page per table group of each list).

VALUES	ATTRIBUTES/TALENTS	PASSIONS
Achievement	Artistic	The arts
Beauty	Athletic	Gaming/Computers
Charity	Adventurous	Writing
Community	Bright	World hunger
Creativity	Brave	Global warming
Collaboration	Charismatic	Humanity
Education	Clever	Sciences
Environment	Compassionate	Social issues
Excellence	Curious	Animal issues
Fairness	Daring	Humanitarian concerns
Family	Dedicated	Medical concerns
Friendship	Energetic	War
Happiness	Focused	Children's rights
Home	Forgiving	Family problems
Humor	Honest	Environment
Imagination	Independent	Oceans
Intelligence	Innovative	Speaking
Intuition	Inquisitive	Creating
Introspection	Leader	Professional sports medicine
Knowledge	Mature	Political reform
Kindness	Motivated	Global water concerns
Leisure	Risk taker	Childhood obesity
Love	Self-reliant	Childhood sports injuries
Money	Sincere	Global education
Purpose	Thoughtful	Artificial intelligence
Skill	Trustworthy	Global collaboration
Solitude	Unique	Building

MISSION POSSIBLE GRAPHIC ORGANIZER

Directions: Complete the table below as indicated in the lesson.

WHAT ARE YOUR TOP FIVE VALUES?	WHAT ARE YOUR TOP FIVE TALENTS/ATTRIBUTES?	WHAT ARE YOUR TOP FIVE PASSIONS?
1.	1.	1.
2.	2.	2.
3.	3.	3.
4.	4.	4.
5.	5.	5.

Use the box below to write a personal statement that brings together your values, talents/attributes, and passions. Remember a strong statement is clearly stated, easy to understand by others, and specific to you:

Example: My purpose is to write inspiring literature and spark imagination and creative spirit in others.

Final Thoughts

Guiding gifted children is not just a job to me, it is my passion. This book represents many of the lessons I have used over the years, as well as the tools I use in my coaching practice. It is my hope that the information can help you be a voice for gifted children and make their social and emotional development a priority within the educational system.

But their learning does not end with this book. Use the information as a springboard for you to develop your own unique ways to connect with and enhance the emotional lives of our gifted youth. Through our efforts, we can change the trajectory for kids—they will learn who they are and redefine what it means to be gifted. Together, we can improve the outcome for many gifted children, helping them achieve more emotional balance. Together, we can show them how to move in the direction of their dreams, creating a better future for themselves and the world.

Finally, I would love to hear from you and your class as you use some of the lessons. Contact me with your own stories and suggestions. I can be reached via e-mail at Christine@christinefonseca.com or on my many social networking sites. Together we can help drastically improve the often complex lives of gifted children.

References

Bisland, A. (2004). Developing leadership skills in young gifted students. *Gifted Child Today, 27*(1), 24–27. Retrieved from http://files.eric.ed.gov/fulltext/EJ682651.pdf

Collaborative for Academic, Social, and Emotional Learning. (2005). *Safe and sound: An educational leader's guide to evidence-based social and emotional learning programs—Illinois edition.* Retrieved from http://static.squarespace.com/static/513f79f9e4b05ce7b70e9673/t/5331c141e4b0fba62007694a/1395769665836/safe-and-sound-il-edition.pdf

Collaborative for Academic, Social, and Emotional Learning. (n.d.). *Social and emotional learning core competencies.* Retrieved from http://www.casel.org/social-and-emotional-learning/core-competencies/

Cross, T. L. (2011). *On the social and emotional lives of gifted children: Issues and factors in their psychological development* (4th ed.). Waco, TX: Prufrock Press.

Day-Vines, N. L., Patton, J. M., Quek, C. G., & Wood, S. (2009). Addressing social-emotional and curricular needs of gifted African-American adolescents. In J. L. VanTassel-Baska, T. L. Cross, & F. R. Olenchak (Eds.), *Social-emotional curriculum with gifted and talented students* (pp. 153–192). Waco, TX: Prufrock Press.

Durlak, J. A., Weissberg, R. P., Dymnicki, A. B., Taylor, R. D., & Schellinger, K. B. (2010). The impact of enhancing students' social and emotional learning: A meta-analysis of school-based universal interventions. *Child Development, 82*(1), 405–432. Retrieved from http://www.thomstecher.com/images/Meta-Analysis-Child-Development-Full-Article.pdf

Fonseca, C. (2011a). *101 success secrets for gifted kids: The ultimate handbook.* Waco, TX: Prufrock Press.

Fonseca, C. (2011b). *Emotional intensity in gifted students: Helping kids cope with explosive feelings.* Waco, TX: Prufrock Press.

Fonseca, C. (2014). *Quiet kids: Help your introverted child succeed in an extroverted world.* Waco, TX: Prufrock Press.

Ford, D. Y. (2006). Creating culturally responsive classrooms for gifted students. *Understanding Our Gifted, 19*(1), 10–14.

Ford, D., Tyson, C., Howard, T., & Harris, J. J. (2000). Multicultural literature and gifted Black students: Promoting self-understanding, awareness, and pride. *Roeper Review, 22,* 235–240. doi:10.1080/02783190009554045

Gagné, F. (2005). From gifts to talents: the DMGT as a developmental model. In R. J. Sternberg, & J. E. Davidson (Eds.), *Conceptions of giftedness* (pp. 98–119). New York, NY: Cambridge University Press.

Grantham, T. C. (2004). Multicultural mentoring to increase Black male representation in gifted programs. *Gifted Child Quarterly, 48,* 232–245. doi:10.1177/001698620404800307

Halsted, J. (2009). *Some of my best friends are books: Guiding gifted readers* (3rd ed.). Scottsdale, AZ: Great Potential Press.

Hébert, T. P. (2009). Guiding gifted teenagers to self-understanding through biography. In J. L. VanTassel-Baska, T. L. Cross, & F. R. Olenchak (Eds.), *Social-emotional curriculum with gifted and talented students* (pp. 259–287). Waco, TX: Prufrock Press.

Hébert, T. P. (2011). *Understanding the social and emotional lives of gifted students.* Waco, TX: Prufrock Press.

Jung, J. Y. (2012). Giftedness as a developmental construct that leads to eminence as adults: Ideas and implications from an occupational/career decision-making perspective. *Gifted Child Quarterly, 56,* 189–193. doi:10.1177/0016986212456072

Jung, J. Y. (2013). The cognitive processes associated with occupational/career indecision: A model for gifted adolescents. *Journal for the Education of the Gifted, 36,* 433–460. doi:10.1177/0162353213506067

Jung, J. Y. (2014). Modeling the occupational/career decision-making processes of intellectually gifted adolescents: A competing models strategy. *Journal for the Education of the Gifted, 37,* 128–152. doi:10.1177/0162353214529045

Kitano, M. K., & Lewis, R. B. (2005). Resilience and coping: Implications for gifted children and youth at risk. *Roeper Review, 27,* 200–205. doi:10.1080/02783190509554319

Kong, T. (2013). *Socioemotional competencies, cognitive ability, and achievement in gifted students.* Doctoral dissertation, Arizona State University. Retrieved from http://repository.asu.edu/attachments/125830/content/Kong_asu_0010E_13451.pdf

Lee, S. Y., & Olszewski-Kubilius, P. (2006). The emotional intelligence, moral judgment, and leadership of academically gifted adolescents. *Journal for the Education of the Gifted, 30,* 29–67. doi:10.1177/016235320603000103

Maxwell, M. (2007). Career counseling is personal counseling: A constructivist approach to nurturing the development of gifted female adolescents. *The Career Development Quarterly, 55,* 206–224. doi:10.1002/j.2161-0045.2007.tb00078.x

Moon, S. M. (2009). Theories to guide affective curriculum development. In J. L. VanTassel-Baska, T. L. Cross, & F. R. Olenchak (Eds.), *Social-emotional curriculum with gifted and talented students* (pp. 11–39). Waco, TX: Prufrock Press.

National Association for Gifted Children. (2010). *NAGC Pre-K–grade 12 gifted education programming standards.* Retrieved from http://www.nagc.org/resources-publications/resources/national-standards-gifted-and-talented-education/pre-k-grade-12

National Governors Association Center for Best Practices, & Council of Chief State School Officers. (2010). *Common Core State Standards for English language arts.* Washington, DC: Authors. Retrieved from http://www.corestandards.org/ELA-Literacy/

Neihart, M. (2002). Risk and resilience in gifted children: A conceptual framework. In M. Neihart, S. M. Reis, N. M. Robinson, & S. M. Moon (Eds.), *The social and emotional development of gifted children: What do we know?* (pp. 113–122). Waco, TX: Prufrock Press.

Neihart, M., Reis, S. M., Robinson, N. M., & Moon, S. M. (2002). *The social and emotional development of gifted children: What do we know?* Waco, TX: Prufrock Press.

Olenchak, F. R. (2009). Creating a life: Orchestrating a symphony of self, a work always in progress. In J. L. VanTassel-Baska, T. L. Cross, & F. R. Olenchak (Eds.), *Social-emotional curriculum with gifted and talented students* (pp. 41–77). Waco, TX: Prufrock Press.

Olszewski-Kubilius P., & Thomson, D. (2015). Talent development as a framework for gifted education. *Gifted Child Today, 38*(1), 49–59.

Peterson, J. S. (2009). Focusing on where they are: A clinical perspective. In J. L. VanTassel-Babka, T. L. Cross, & F. R. Olenchak (Eds.), *Social-emotional curriculum with gifted and talented students* (pp. 193–226). Waco, TX: Prufrock Press.

Peterson, J. S., & Lorimer, M. R. (2011). Student response to a small-group affective curriculum in a school for gifted children. *Gifted Child Quarterly, 55,* 167–180. doi:10.1177/0016986211412770

Peterson, J. S., Betts, G., & Bradley, T. (2009). Discussion groups as a component of affective curriculum for gifted students. In J. L. VanTassel-Baska, T. L. Cross, & F. R. Olenchak (Eds.), *Social-emotional curriculum with gifted and talented students* (pp. 289–320). Waco, TX: Prufrock Press.

Prince-Embury, S. (2005). *Resiliency scale for adolescents: A profile of personal strengths.* San Antonio, TX: Pearson Education.

Pyryt, M. C. (2003). Technology and the gifted. In N. Colangelo & G. A. Davis (Eds.), *Handbook of gifted education* (3rd ed., pp. 582–589). Boston, MA: Allyn & Bacon.

Reis, S. M., & Renzulli, J. S. (2004). Current research on the social and emotional development of gifted and talented students: Good news and future possibilities. *Psychology in schools, 41*(1), 130. Retrieved from http://pearsonflipbook. aptaracorp.com/0-328-73631-7/data/r11_nl_en_rbase_artcl21.pdf

Renzulli, J. S. (1978). What makes giftedness? Reexamining a definition. *Phi Delta Kappan, 60,* 180–184.

Renzulli, J. S. (2005). The three-ring conception of giftedness: A developmental model for promoting creative productivity. In R. J. Sternberg & J. E. Davidson (Eds.), *Conceptions of giftedness* (pp. 246–279). New York, NY: Cambridge University Press.

Renzulli, J. S. (2009). Operation Houndstooth: A positive perspective of developing social intelligence. In J. L. VanTassel-Baska, T. L. Cross, & F. R. Olenchak (Eds.), *Social-emotional curriculum with gifted and talented students* (pp. 79–112). Waco, TX: Prufrock Press.

Renzulli, J. S. (2012). Reexamining the role of gifted education and talent development for the 21st century: A four-part theorectical approach. *Gifted Child Quarterly, 56,* 150–159. Retrieved from http://scottbarrykaufman.com/wp-content/up loads/2012/06/GCQ-article-Reexamining-Role-of-Gifted-Ed-and-Talent-Dev1. pdf

Siegle, D. (2013). *The underachieving gifted child: Recognizing, understanding, and reversing underachievement.* Waco, TX: Prufrock Press.

Silverman, L. K. (2007). Perfectionism: The crucible of giftedness. *Gifted Education International, 23,* 233–245. doi:10.1177/026142940702300304

Stewart, J. B. (2007). Career counseling for the academically gifted student. *Canadian Journal of Counselling and Psychotherapy, 33*(1). Retrieved from http://www.cjc-rcc.ucalgary.ca/cjc/index.php/rcc/article/viewFile/126/307

VanTassel-Baska, J. L. (2009). Affective curriculum and instruction for gifted learners. In J. L. VanTassel-Baska, T. L. Cross, & F. R. Olenchak (Eds.), *Social-emotional curriculum with gifted and talented students* (pp. 113–132). Waco, TX: Prufrock Press.

VanTassel-Baska, J. L., Buckingham, B. L., & Baska, A. (2009). The role of the arts in the socioemotional development of the gifted. In J. L. VanTassel-Baska, T. L. Cross, & F. R. Olenchak (Eds.), *Social-emotional curriculum with gifted and talented students* (pp. 227–257). Waco, TX: Prufrock Press.

Webb, J. T., Gore, J. L., Amend, E. R., & DeVries, A. R. (2007). *A parent's guide to gifted children.* Scottsdale, AZ: Great Potential Press.

Wilcox, E. (2013). *Advising high achievers, gifted learners and creative thinkers.* Retrieved from http://advisingmatters.berkeley.edu/sites/default/files/re-edited_ Final_Advising%20High%20Achievers_EW-12_09_13%20(2)_0.pdf

Standards Tables

TABLE A.1
SELECTED NAGC STANDARDS

STANDARD	STUDENT OUTCOMES	EVIDENCE-BASED PRACTICES
Standard 1: Learning and Development	1.1 Self-Understanding: Demonstrate self-knowledge with respect to interests, strengths, identities and needs in social-emotional development.	1.1.1 Assist students in identifying strengths, interests and talents.
	1.2 Self-Understanding: Demonstrate an understanding of how they learn and grow.	1.2.1 Match activities to students' developmental and cultural learning needs.
	1.3 Self-Understanding: Demonstrate an understanding of similarities and differences between themselves and various peer groups.	1.3.1 Use research-based grouping practices to enable students to interact with diverse individuals.
	1.4 Awareness of Needs: Access to resources within the community to support social-emotional needs and interests.	1.4.1 Provide role models through mentoring, bibliotherapy and similar practices that align with student interests. 1.4.2 Identify potential out-of-school opportunities.
	1.6 Cognitive and Affective Growth: Access to challenging learning activities that address their unique needs.	1.6.1 Use research-based strategies. 1.6.2 Provide research-based interventions for underachievers or twice-exceptional.

STANDARD	STUDENT OUTCOMES	EVIDENCE-BASED PRACTICES
Standard 1: Learning and Development, *continued*	1.7 Cognitive and Affective Growth: Identify preferred approaches to learning and expand their repertoire.	1.7.1 Assist students in identifying preferred approaches to learning. Accommodate preferences while increasing exposure to new ways of learning.
	1.8 Cognitive and Affective Growth: Match interests and talents to career goals. Access resources to assist with goals.	1.8.1 Provide college and career guidance. 1.8.2 Include curriculum that focuses on social awareness and adjustment, as well as career awareness.
Standard 3: Curriculum Planning and Instruction	3.2 Talent Development: Increase mastery in multiple talent/interest areas and across a variety of learning opportunities.	3.1.1 Develop and utilize challenging affective, social and leadership curriculum.
	3.3 Talent Development: Increase mastery in specific areas of interest.	3.3.3 Provide opportunities to explore, develop and research areas of interest and/or talent.
	3.4 Instructional Strategies: Become an "independent investigator", utilizing critical and creative thinking and problem-solving skills.	3.4.1 Teach and utilize critical thinking strategies. 3.4.2 Teach and utilize creative-thinking strategies. 3.4.3 Teach and utilize problem-solving strategies. 3.4.4 Teach and utilize inquiry method strategies.
	3.5 Culturally Relevant Curriculum: Develop knowledge and skills for living in a global, diverse society.	3.5.1 Utilize a culturally responsive and challenging curriculum. 3.5.2 Integrate career exploration experiences through biography and speakers. 3.5.3 All for deep exploration of diversity, including language, culture and social issues.

STANDARD	STUDENT OUTCOMES	EVIDENCE-BASED PRACTICES
Standard 4: Learning Environments	4.1 Personal Competence: Demonstrate growth in the areas of self-awareness, self-advocacy, self-efficacy, confidence, motivation, resilience, independence, curiosity, and risk taking.	4.1.2 Provide opportunities for self-exploration and the pursuit of interests. 4.1.5 Provide positive examples of coping skills and application.
	4.2 Social Competence: Develop social competence through positive peer relationships and social interactions.	4.2.1 Provide opportunities to interact with a variety of peer groups. 4.2.3 Provide instruction on social skills.
	4.3 Leadership: Demonstrate personal and social responsibility and leadership.	4.3.1 Establish a safe environment for all students. 4.3.2 Provide opportunities to develop leadership skills. 4.3.3 Provide opportunities to effect positive change in a variety of environments.
	4.4 Cultural Competence: Demonstrate strong communication and collaboration skills within a diverse population. Apply these skills to address social issues.	4.4.1 Model cultural sensitivity within the classroom. 4.4.3 Provide opportunities to collaborate with diverse peers on common goals.
	4.5 Communication Competence: Develop interpersonal and technical communication skills, including oral, written and creative communication. Demonstrate fluency with technologies that support communication.	4.5.2 Provide resources to enhance all forms of communication, including oral, written and artistic. 4.5.3 Provide access to advanced communication tools to express higher-thinking and creativity.
Standard 5: Programming	5.7 Career Pathways: Identify future career goals and pathways for achieving goals.	5.7.1 Provide guidance counseling.

Note. Adapted from *Pre-K–Grade 12 Gifted Education Programming Standards* by National Association for Gifted Children, 2010, Washington, DC: Author. Retrieved from http://www.nagc.org/resources-publications/resources/national-standards-gifted-and-talented-education/pre-k-grade-12.

TABLE A.2
SOCIAL-EMOTIONAL LEARNING SKILLS

COMPETENCY	RELATED SKILLS
Self-awareness	Identify emotions Self-confidence Self-efficacy
Self-management	Impulse control Stress management Self-discipline Motivation Goal setting Organization skills
Social-awareness	Perspective taking Empathy Diversity training Respect for self and others
Relationship skills	Communication Social engagement Relationships Cooperation Conflict resolution Self-advocacy
Responsible decision making	Problem-solving skills Social and personal responsibility

Note. Adapted from *Social and emotional learning core competencies*, by Collaborative for Academic, Social, and Emotional Learning. (n.d.). Retrieved from http://www.casel.org/social-and-emotional-learning/core-competencies/

TABLE A.3
COMMON CORE STATE STANDARDS FOR ENGLISH LANGUAGE ARTS-LITERACY: K–12 COLLEGE AND CAREER READINESS ANCHOR STANDARDS

ANCHOR STANDARD	STUDENT OUTCOMES
Reading: Key Ideas and details	
CCSS.ELA-Literacy.CCRA.R.3	Analyze the development of ideas and the interaction of ideas, event and individuals in text.
Reading: Integration of knowledge and ideas	
CCSS.ELA-Literacy.CCRA.R.7	Evaluate text presented in diverse media and formats, including qualitative and visual information.

ANCHOR STANDARD	STUDENT OUTCOMES
CCSS.ELA-Literacy.CCRA.R.8	Evaluate specific claims in text, including validity of reasoning and sufficiency of evidence.
Writing: Text types and purposes	
CCSS.ELA-Literacy.CCRA.W.1	Write text to support claims in analysis of topics using valid reasoning and sufficient evidence.
CCSS.ELA-Literacy.CCRA.W.2	Write informative text to examine complex ideas and information through the effective selection and organization of content.
CCSS.ELA-Literacy.CCRA.W.3	Write narratives to develop experiences (nonfiction or fiction) using well-structured sequences and details.
Writing: Production and distribution of writing	
CCSS.ELA-Literacy.CCRA.W.4	Produce coherent writing appropriate to task, purpose and audience.
CCSS.ELA-Literacy.CCRA.W.6	Use technology to produce and publish writing, and to collaborate with others.
Writing: Research to build and present knowledge	
CCSS.ELA-Literacy.CCRA.W.7	Conduct varied research projects based on focus questions which demonstrate understanding of the subject matter.
CCSS.ELA-Literacy.CCRA.W.8	Gather, evaluate and utilize information from multiple print and digital sources.
CCSS.ELA-Literacy.CCRA.W.9	Draw evidence from varied text to support research and opinion.
Listening and Speaking: Comprehension and Collaboration	
CCSS.ELA-Literacy.CCRA.SL.1	Effectively engage in a variety of conversations and collaborations with diverse partners.
CCSS.ELA-Literacy.CCRA.SL.2	Evaluate information presented in diverse media and formats.
CCSS.ELA-Literacy.CCRA.SL.3	Evaluate a speaker's point of view and reasoning.

ANCHOR STANDARD	STUDENT OUTCOMES
Listening and Speaking: Presentation of knowledge and ideas	
CCSS.ELA-Literacy.CCRA.SL.4	Present information, including supporting evidence, effectively and appropriate to task, purpose, and audience.
CCSS.ELA-Literacy.CCRA.SL.5	Utilize digital media and visual displays to express information during presentations.
CCSS.ELA-Literacy.CCRA.SL.6	Adapt speech to a variety of communication tasks.
Language: Conventions of Standard English	
CCSS.ELA-Literacy.CCRA.L.1	Demonstrate appropriate use of language conventions for grammar when writing and speaking.
CCSS.ELA-Literacy.CCRA.L.2	Demonstrate appropriate use of language conventions for capitalization and punctuation when writing.
Language: Knowledge of language	
CCSS.ELA-Literacy.CCRA.L.3	Apply knowledge of language usage to understand how language functions in different contexts and to utilize it appropriately when speaking, and comprehend it more deeply when reading or listening.
Language: Vocabulary acquisition and use	
CCSS.ELA-Literacy.CCRA.L.6	Acquire and accurately use a variety of academic and domain-specific vocabulary when reading, writing, speaking, and listening.

Note. Adapted from *Common Core State Standards for English language arts*, National Governors Association Center for Best Practices & Council of Chief State School Officers, 2010, Washington, DC: Authors. Retrieved from http://www.corestandards. org/ELA-Literacy/

About Christine Fonseca

Critically acclaimed and award-winning nonfiction and fiction author **Christine Fonseca** is dedicated to helping children and adults find their unique voice in the world. In nonfiction, she delves into the world of giftedness, resiliency, and temperament, offering children and adults a no-nonsense, how-to approach to facing the world without fear. She has taught parenting classes for more than a decade, works with educators to understand the social and emotional needs of the gifted, and is a frequent presenter at statewide conferences on topics related to children and education. Christine works as a school psychologist in the elementary, middle, and high school levels. She also coaches children and parents to work through their anxieties.

Christine has written self-help articles for Parents.com, Johnson & Johnson, *Bop/Tiger Beat*, and *Justine Magazine*. She was awarded a 2013 Special Achievement Award from the Surrey International Writer's Conference for her body of work and efforts to give back to the community, and was a semifinalist in the Kindle Book Review's Best Indie Book (Young Adult) for her thriller, *Transcend*. Recent titles include *Quiet Kids*, *Raising the Shy Child*, *Indie and Proud*, and the YA suspense series, *The Solomon Experiments*.

Christine lives in the San Diego area with her husband and children. When she isn't crafting new books, she can be found sipping too many skinny vanilla lattes at the local coffee house, or exploring the world with her family. For more information about Christine or her books, visit her website http://christinefonseca.com.